YORK NO[T]

General Editors: Profes
of Stirling) & Professor
University of Beirut)

Graham Greene

THE POWER
AND
THE GLORY

Notes by Adele King

BA (IOWA) MA (LEEDS) DU (PARIS)

LONGMAN
YORK PRESS

YORK PRESS
Immeuble Esseily, Place Riad Solh, Beirut.

LONGMAN GROUP UK LIMITED
Longman House, Burnt Mill, Harlow,
Essex CM20 2JE, England
Associated companies, branches and representatives
throughout the world

First published 1982
Fourth impression 1989

ISBN 0-582-03352-7

Produced by Longman Group (FE) Ltd.
Printed in Hong Kong

Contents

Part 1

Introduction

Life of Graham Greene

Graham Greene was born on 2 October 1904 at Berkhamsted, Hertfordshire, where his father, D.H. Greene, was headmaster of Berkhamsted School, an English public school (privately supported, not a government school). Greene's childhood, which he has described in several essays and in his autobiography *A Sort of Life* (1971), was an intense, imaginative period; he has often expressed the view that all one's life is determined by childhood experiences, that a novelist is formed during his first sixteen years. After growing up as part of a large, educated family, he became a boarder at his father's school. He was a sensitive child, whose boarding school days were often tortured by bullies, and who was early aware of a connection between pain and sexual pleasure. Life seemed full of dangers and betrayal. Boarding school, he said, taught him the meaning of hell; he believed in hell before he believed in heaven. He responded readily to such childhood reading as Rider Haggard's (1856–1925) *King Solomon's Mines* (1885) and especially Marjorie Bowen's (1886–1952) *Viper of Milan* (1917), which gave him a picture of 'perfect evil walking the world where perfect good can never walk again'.* Greene's imagination was fired in his childhood by the conflict between the powers of good and the powers of evil, and by a sense of the corruption and the suffering of man. He remembers, from his early childhood, walking with a servant past a house where a man had just committed suicide; later he learned of a local girl who finding herself pregnant lay on a railway track to kill herself.

He suffered from depressions. When he was sixteen, his parents sent him to London for psychoanalytical treatment, which resulted in a feeling of calmness, but also an increasing sense of the banality of everyday life. He fought off boredom by reading and later by unsuccessful attempts at suicide. At the age of nineteen, he sometimes played Russian roulette, putting one bullet in a revolver, spinning the cartridge and firing against his head, giving himself a one in six chance of being killed.

Greene read history at Balliol College, Oxford, from 1922 to 1925.

Collected Essays, Bodley Head, London, 1969, p.18.

Like many of his contemporaries, he was interested in the revolutionary politics of the era and was, very briefly, a member of the Communist Party. While never a serious Marxist, Greene has always shown sympathy for the poor, the victims of society. Many years later, in 1955, after an interview with Ho Chi Minh in Indo-China, Greene wrote: 'the anonymous peasant has never been treated so like an individual before... There is something in Communism besides the politics.'* While interviewing Fidel Castro in Cuba in 1966 Greene was to argue for the possibility of co-operation between Catholicism and Communism.

When still a student, Greene published *Babbling April*, a book of poems, but he soon abandoned poetry for fiction. At Oxford he also met a Roman Catholic girl whom he was to marry in 1927. In 1926, while working as a reporter in Nottingham, he was received into the Roman Catholic Church. He has described his adherence to Catholicism as essentially intellectual. The emotional basis for his religious beliefs can be traced back to his childhood experiences of the 'hell' of boarding school.

After several years as a sub-editor with *The Times* in London, Greene published a novel, *The Man Within*, in 1929. (It was the third he had written.) It sold eight thousand copies. He was offered a contract and a limited regular income by the publishing firm of Heinemann, and decided to devote himself to writing. Several novels were published in quick succession, but it was only with the appearance of *Stamboul Train* in 1932 that Greene began to establish a reputation. He classified *Stamboul Train* as an 'entertainment'. For some years he divided his fiction into 'entertainments', which were basically adventure stories, and 'novels', which were more serious, with more profound character analysis. The division is, however, rather arbitrary, as all his works reflect similar preoccupations with the plight of contemporary man in a hostile and lonely world, but a world in which the power of God works in often mysterious ways. Among books Greene published in the 1930s that brought him considerable fame are *England Made Me* (1935) and *A Gun for Sale* (American title: *This Gun for Hire*, 1936). In 1934 he made a trip to Liberia and Sierra Leone, which he described in *Journey Without Maps* (1936).

The first of his novels with a specifically religious theme, *Brighton Rock*, appeared in 1938. At this time he was film critic for *The Spectator* in London. One of his articles, criticising a film featuring the popular child actress Shirley Temple, was judged libellous. Partly to avoid the unpleasant publicity resulting from the judgement, Greene travelled to Mexico in 1938 to report on religious persecution there. In

Collected Essays, p.404.

1939 he published a travel book on Mexico, *The Lawless Roads*, and in 1940 *The Power and the Glory*, a novel based on his Mexican experience.

During the Second World War he worked for the British Foreign Office and was stationed in Sierra Leone. The third of his group of Catholic novels, *The Heart of the Matter*, published in 1948, is set in Sierra Leone. Greene has travelled widely as a journalist. He was in Kenya and Malaya in 1951, and in Indo-China in 1954. From this latter trip came *The Quiet American* (1955).

In 1949 Greene wrote the script for *The Third Man*, a film about spy intrigues in Vienna. He had long been interested in the cinema and had written a film script for his novel *Brighton Rock* in 1948. *The Third Man* enjoyed a large international success. He also began writing for the stage. His first play to be performed in London, *The Living Room*, was produced and published in 1953. Although his fiction is often influenced by dramatic and especially by cinematic techniques, most critics have agreed that his plays are below the level of his fiction.

Among Greene's works since the 1950s are *Our Man in Havana* (1958), his only novel with a happy ending; *A Burnt-Out Case* (1961), which followed a trip to the Congo in 1959; *The Comedians* (1966), set in Haiti; *Travels with My Aunt* (1969); and *The Human Factor* (1978), based loosely on the defection of several former British foreign officers to the Soviet Union. Greene has often used incidents of recent political and social history as the basis of his work.

Although now in his eighties, he continues to write prolifically. Recent novels include *Doctor Fischer of Geneva or The Bomb Party* (1980) and *Monsignor Quixote* (1983). Non-fiction includes *J'accuse: Nice, the Dark Side* (1982) and *Getting to Know the General* (1984). He has also published a second volume of autobiography, *Ways of Escape* (1980). Greene has stated that he is no longer preoccupied with religion and in his recent work he has turned his attention to secular concerns.

Graham Greene and Roman Catholicism

It is evident from his autobiographical writings that Greene's imagination is based on childhood experience many years before his conversion to Catholicism. He is especially concerned with the corruption of man and the strangeness of God's mercy, which appears at unlikely moments, often to people whose lives are not conventionally religious or moral. His work expresses a personal vision. *The Power and the Glory* was condemned by the Church because it was not considered orthodox in its presentation of Catholic beliefs. Greene recounts in *A Sort of Life* how he refused to make changes in the novel. Later Pope Paul told him that he had read the novel and added: 'Some parts of all your books will always offend some Catholics. You should not worry about that.'*

In the twentieth century, however, when many prominent novelists have been agnostic or disinterested in religion, and in Britain, where Catholicism is a minority faith, Greene's novels are unusual because they reflect his Catholic belief. Catholicism provides him with a system of concepts and a set of symbols through which he expresses his vision of life. His main characters are usually Catholic. Because they should be aware of the presence of God, they are treated differently and often more harshly than the non-Catholics in his novels. A sense of the mysterious presence of God in the temporal world and of the power of the sacraments of the Church underlies Greene's fiction, and particularly what is often referred to as his 'Catholic trilogy': *Brighton Rock*, *The Power and the Glory* and *The Heart of the Matter*. Thus while Greene has said that he is not a Catholic novelist, in the sense of a propagandist for his religion, he is surely a novelist whose faith has profoundly influenced his work.

The Mexican Revolution

When Greene went to Mexico to write on religious persecution, the Mexican Revolution had been underway since 1911. The Constitution of 1917 included many anti-clerical measures. The churches became state property, religious processions were banned, clerical dress was forbidden on the streets. These laws were, however, laxly applied until the presidency of Plutarco Elias Calles, who in 1926 began persecution of the Catholics. Churches were closed, foreign clergy were deported and saying Mass or performing the sacraments became a serious offence. The bishops ordered priests to withdraw, expecting the government to give in, but it did not. For three years there was much violence on both sides; Catholic guerrillas were repressed brutally by soldiers. After Calles was replaced in 1934 by his rival, Lázaro Cárdenas, anti-Catholic laws continued to be enforced in all states of Mexico except San Luis Potosí; but a few priests were allowed to serve in some states and laws were slackly enforced in tourist areas, particularly the District of Mexico City. In 1937 peasants in Vera Cruz forced open the churches after a child had been killed by the police on his way home from Mass.

In Tabasco and Chiapas, southern Mexican states near the Guatemalan border, active persecution continued. The fanatic dictator in Tabasco, Tomás Garrido Canabal, and his followers, the 'Red Shirts', pulled down many churches. Garrido Canabal was a minister

A Sort of Life, Bodley Head, London, 1971, p.77.

in the Mexican government in 1934 but, before Greene's arrival in Mexico in 1938, he had been given a diplomatic post abroad. Although his hold on Tabasco gradually broke down, in 1938 in Villahermosa, the capital city of Tabasco, the police fired on a crowd of peasants setting up an altar. In most of the state of Chiapas, no churches were open; the bishop was in exile. In Las Casas, however, churches were open, but priests were not allowed to enter them.

During Greene's travels in Mexico, he saw peasants praying in the churches without priests, and he attended Masses in rooms where the sanctus bell could not be rung for fear of the police. Shortly after he left Mexico, however, the Bishop of Tabasco was allowed to return and a truce was established between church and state.

A note on the text

The Power and the Glory (Graham Greene's tenth novel) was published by William Heinemann Ltd, London, in 1940. It was first published in the United States in 1940 under the title, *The Labyrinthine Ways*. Although his first novel had sold well, *The Power and the Glory* had an initial printing of only three and a half thousand copies. It did not sell well during the war years, but was very successful later. It was also published in a French translation, with an introduction by the well-known French novelist François Mauriac (1885–1970), and was widely acclaimed by French critics.

The book has been republished, with an introduction by Greene, as Volume 5 in the collected edition of his works by William Heinemann and Bodley Head, London, 1971. It was first published by Penguin Books, Harmondsworth, in 1962 and has been reprinted many times. In 1971 it was reset and reprinted from the collected edition of Greene's work. The York Notes are based on the 1971 Penguin Books edition.

The Power and the Glory has twice been filmed. The first version, directed by John Ford and starring Henry Fonda as the whisky priest, was released in 1947. Greene was disturbed by the film, in which the priest has integrity and the atheist lieutenant is corrupt, a reversal of the novel. In the second version, made by Laurence Olivier in 1967, the ending was changed; there is no appearance of a new priest to replace the whisky priest after his execution. *The Power and the Glory* was also dramatised for the stage in 1956.

Part 2

Summaries

of THE POWER AND THE GLORY

A general summary

In the state of Tabasco, Mexico, where religion has been outlawed, all priests have fled or been killed except Padre José, who has married his housekeeper and renounced performing any religious rites, and a whisky priest, a stubborn man who has continued in his vocation, although he has given up observing most of his duties. He is often drunk and has even fathered a child. As the novel opens, Mr Tench, an English dentist, meets the priest, who gives up his chance to escape when he is summoned to the bed of a woman supposedly dying. A police lieutenant, who hates the Church for its oppression of the poor, vows to hunt down the last priest by taking hostages from the villages. He will kill them if the priest's movements are not reported.

The priest hides temporarily at a banana station run by an Englishman, Captain Fellows, whose daughter Coral befriends him. He then returns to the village where his child lives. He feels a great love for her, but she rejects him. When the police come searching for him in the village, he is not betrayed and a hostage is taken. After this, he feels he cannot stay in any place except the capital city. While travelling there he meets a half-caste, who recognises he is a priest and hopes to betray him for a reward. After buying wine for the Mass, the priest gets caught with a bottle of illegal brandy and is imprisoned for a night. Although he identifies himself to the other prisoners, he is not betrayed.

Trying to escape across the border to another state, the priest stops at the Fellows's home and finds it abandoned. He later learns that James Calver, an American gangster whom the police are also seeking, has been in the area and taken an Indian child to use as a shield. The priest helps the Indian mother take the dead child to be buried at the foot of a cross. Feverish, he stumbles on, expecting to die, but he reaches the border of the next state and is safe from the police. He stays at the home of the Lehrs, says a Mass and hears confessions. As he is about to journey on to the city of Las Casas, where churches are still open, the half-caste arrives with a note from Calver, who is dying and wants to confess. Although he realises it is a trick to lure him back across the border, as a priest he cannot refuse. Calver dies trying to give the priest a knife to defend himself. The lieutenant then arrests him. As they debate their conflicting views of life on the journey back to the capital, each man comes to respect the other. The lieutenant even breaks his strict discipline to try, unsuccessfully, to persuade Padre José to give the priest confession before his execution. The priest dies thinking his life has been useless. After his death, however, Coral's father mentions how much she was influenced by the priest; Mr Tench has a letter from his estranged wife saying she has forgiven him; Luis, a young boy who was bored by his mother's story of Juan the Martyr and who secretly admired the lieutenant, suddenly sees the whisky priest as a hero. Then, unexpectedly, a new priest for Tabasco arrives at Luis's home.

Detailed summaries

Part I, Chapter 1: The Port

Mr Tench, an English dentist practising in a small Mexican town, walks to the quay to get an ether cylinder from an incoming boat. He meets a small man, a Mexican who speaks English and who is looking at the boat with interest. Mr Tench invites him home so they can share the stranger's brandy. With some pride, he shows the stranger his dental equipment. Their conversation is interrupted by the arrival of a child looking for a doctor for his dying mother. The stranger feels impelled to go with the child. When they leave, Mr Tench realises he forgot to get his ether cylinder and feels abandoned. The stranger, riding a mule to the child's mother, also feels abandoned.

The opening chapter, told from the point of view of Mr Tench, both sets the scene of abandonment and desolation and introduces, indirectly, the central character, the whisky priest. Only from a few hints in his conversation can the reader guess that he is a priest.

NOTES AND GLOSSARY:

The Port: Frontera, not named in the novel

Mr Tench went out: the opening paragraph is justly famous for establishing economically the atmosphere of heat, decay, abandon and death that pervades the Mexican landscape in which the novel is set: 'blazing Mexican sun', 'bleaching dust', 'vultures', 'shabby indifference', 'carrion'. The scene is presented from the perspective of Mr Tench, who is characterised as weak and ineffectual: 'faint feeling of rebellion', 'splintering fingernails', 'feebly'.

ex-president, ex-general, ex-human being: the description of the statue reduces political and military ambitions to their timeless unimportance; they lead only to death

Buenos dias: (*Spanish*) 'good morning'

a man with a gun: the violent atmosphere of the town is indicated

But it wasn't like England: Mr Tench is out of place in Mexico, home-sick, abandoned

The Treasury which had once been a church: the first indication of the state suppression of religion that forms the political setting of the action

he suddenly forgot what he had come out for: a detail portraying Mr Tench as a confused individual, but also with a deeper resonance, suggesting that Mr Tench has no real purpose in his life

It didn't really matter: everybody was insured when he bought a ticket: an ironic comment on the value a materialistic society places on human life

that was how one lived, putting off everything: Mr Tench has abandoned any sense of purpose in his life

Cerveza Moctezuma: a Mexican beer

they were generally so thick: Mr Tench's judgement on Mexican women, whom he sees as essentially different from himself

Somebody: the first mention of the whisky priest, who is never named in the novel. Here he appears as an indistinct, rather disreputable character, of 'unstable hilarity', presumably from drinking. He assumes Tench's muttering is addressed to him, perhaps because he heard 'My God'. The significance of this would not, of course, be apparent on first reading

seemed to evade the question: the priest would like to leave on the ship, but cannot bring himself to admit it

any medicine . . . for—oh, hell: ironically, the priest does have medicine for 'hell'. Often the seeming profanity in the novel also has a literal meaning

Ora pro nobis: 'pray for us', part of the Latin Mass

Lopez: the discussion of Lopez, shot for helping people escape, strengthens the reader's feeling that this 'little man' is engaged in some illegal activity. This is in surprising contrast with a distressed facial expression Tench notices when he mentions Lopez's mistress

his first memory: early childhood memories are always significant for Greene, as he believes that a child's first impressions set the tone of his imagination and the pattern of his life

Pride wavered in his voice like a plant with shallow roots: typical of Greene's similes, comparing an abstract quality with a concrete object

stained glass: the stranger admires the Madonna in the glass, another hint to his identity

death was in his carious mouth already: a premonition of the end of the novel

The brown eyes expressed no emotion: this nameless child is the first of a series of children in the novel, all of whom seem prematurely aware of suffering

as though unwillingly he had been summoned to an occasion he couldn't pass by: the child's arrival, it seems, is an act of God preventing the priest's escape from Tabasco. He himself sees it as such ('I am meant to miss it') and feels powerless and angry, 'shaken by a tiny rage'

you do no good: the priest, drunk and confused, takes Mr Tench's comment about doctors as an attack on the priesthood

La Eterna Mártir: 'the eternal martyr'. Under the cover of a cheap novel, the priest has hidden his breviary. Ironically, the title seems to refer to the priest's role rather than to the woman on the novel's cover. Greene saw an advertisement for a film in Mexico called '*Quién Es la Eterna Mártir?*' (Who is the Eternal Martyr?') and contrasted the subject of the film with the passion of Christ*

I am happy: the young girl singing forms a striking contrast to Mr Tench. Her happiness is, however, produced by lack of consciousness of the sorrows of life: 'without considering why'

abandoned: the priest, like Mr Tench, feels abandoned, unwilling to accept God's purpose

when the world spun off into space: images of the creation of the world recur frequently in the priest's and in Padre José's thoughts

like the King of a West African tribe: a reference to tribes on the Guinea coast (which Greene had visited), where the king is often transformed into a semi-divine personnage, whose every action is circumscribed lest by breaking taboos he bring disaster on his people

The Lawless Roads, Heinemann and Bodley Head, London, 1978, p.23.

Part I, Chapter 2: The Capital

Chapter 2 begins with the point of view of the lieutenant, who lives a pure, austere life dedicated to the suppression of all religion. Hearing that the last priest in the state has been sighted, the lieutenant plans to take hostages from the villages in order to catch him. The scene then shifts to a home where a mother reads smuggled stories of martyred priests to her children. Her son is quickly bored with the sentimental piety. Another shift in scene presents Padre José, the only married priest, an old man who feels totally abandoned in sin and wishes he could have had the courage to be shot rather than endure the taunts of the woman he was forced to marry.

NOTES AND GLOSSARY:

The Capital: The town, not named, is Villahermosa. The name in Spanish means 'beautiful city'

He might have been chained to them unwillingly: a first implicit comparison between the lieutenant and the priest; both are chained to duties. The lieutenant, however, is then contrasted in appearance to the priest, for his 'gaiters were polished'

excusados: (*Spanish*) euphemism for 'toilets'

jefe: (*Spanish*) 'chief'

a stout man with a pink fat face: Chief of Police contrasts physically with the lieutenant, who has 'a lean dancer's face'. This contrast reflects their characters; the Chief of Police is easy-going, the lieutenant stern and ascetic

Toothache: this is a link between the Chief and Mr Tench, which will become significant at the end of the novel

James Calver: the first mention of the American robber whose story is frequently linked to the priest's throughout the novel. In this chapter their photographs are compared

The good things of life had come to him too early: the lieutenant's judgement of the priest will be echoed in the priest's own opinion of his past life in Part II, Chapter 1

gringo: Mexican slang term, meaning citizens of the United States. The references to the priest's ability to speak English and to his mule establish that the stranger of Chapter 1 is the same man, the last priest in the state

he remembered the smell of incense in the churches of his boyhood: like Mr Tench's, the lieutenant's perspective is based on his early memories. He sees the Church as adding to the misery of the peasants

he felt no need of women: ironically, the lieutenant lives a pure, more ascetic life than the priest

A man like that . . . does no real harm: the lieutenant's speech, intended to shock by his seeming approval of Calver, shows that he has principles of his own: 'a kind of virtue' in his hatred of the Church

something of a priest . . . a theologian . . . a monastic cell: in his dedication to his cause, the lieutenant is again compared to a priest. His faith is in 'a dying, cooling world' with 'no purpose'

one man had conformed: a first mention of Padre José, shortly before his appearance in the story. (In spite of the disconnected series of episodes in the opening chapters, Greene gives the reader clues to understanding the plot)

with an expression of intense weariness: Luis, the fourteen-year-old boy who will play a significant role later in the novel, is a disillusioned, prematurely wise child

Young Juan: the story of the martyred priest forms an ironic counterpart to the story of the whisky priest. Juan acts like a saint from his childhood; his story is told with 'sweet piety'

that whisky priest: the first mention of the term by which the priest is known. Luis's mother can see no connection between him and Juan the Martyr. Her husband, more realistically, judges that at least the whisky priest 'carries on'

abandoned: Luis's father echoes the feelings of Tench and the priest in Chapter 1

abandoned ship: Padre José also feels abandoned. Greene intends the reader to feel that God is present, however, in this abandoned world

like a galley-slave: Padre José feels chained to his wife, much as the lieutenant is 'chained' to his soldiers

the gift . . . which nobody could take away: according to Catholic doctrine the priest, regardless of his sins or his abjuration of his calling, always retains the power to turn the bread and wine of the Mass into the body and blood of God

the whole abandoned star: note the repetition of 'abandoned'

Part I, Chapter 3: The River

Captain Fellows, an easy-going Englishman on his banana plantation, returns home from work to find the lieutenant searching for the priest. He then learns that his daughter Coral has hidden the priest. Although she thinks in terms of a game, she instinctively wants to help the priest, and arranges for him to signal to her if he returns. The priest travels on to a very poor village, where he only wants to sleep, but is forced to hear the confessions of the peasants.

NOTES AND GLOSSARY:

He was a happy man: a contrast is immediately implied between Captain Fellows and the characters introduced in the first two chapters. Happiness, for Fellows, however, means 'no responsibility for anyone'. He felt happy as well 'in wartime France', a shocking statement in the light of the horrors of trench warfare in the First World War, indicative of the moral blindness of Fellows in contrast to the concern of both the priest and the lieutenant

he was at home anywhere: Fellows's communion with nature is 'shallow' and he thus feels at home in the world, in contrast to all those who feel 'abandoned'

his boots ground peace into the floor: another typical Greene metaphor, comparing the abstract to the concrete

with a look of immense responsibility: Coral, like the Mexican children, has already experienced life's limitations and problems: 'That was what the sun did to a child.' In comparison to Coral, her father seems 'a boy'

he was aware of an inordinate love: as does the priest, Fellows loves his daughter greatly. Neither man, however, has any real contact with or control over his daughter

I know about politics. Mother and I are doing the Reform Bill: Coral's formal education, through correspondence courses, has been limited. What connection there might be between the Mexican Revolution and the English Reform Bill (the bill in 1832 that extended the suffrage by lowering the property qualifications) is presumably beyond her understanding. She has, however, an immediate grasp of the seriousness of the priest's situation

Quién es usted?: (*Spanish*) Who are you?

Begging for brandy: Fellows immediately understands that the priest is an alcoholic

dreaming of weddings: Mrs Fellows is sentimental, living in a false world of romance far removed from reality

carried like children in a coach through the huge spaces without any knowledge of their destination: the image recalls Padre José's speculations about the Earth rolling 'heavily in space'. Padre José, however, knows the destination; he believes in heaven and hell

'She didn't need me,' he said bitterly: the priest is torn between feeling God 'summoned' him and resenting how little he can accomplish

'Unworthy of what?' He clasped his little attaché case: the priest's gesture indicates that he feels unworthy of saying the Mass, the elements of which he carries in the case

answers as plain and understandable as her questions: the priest and Coral, removed from the usual complications of adult social life, can communicate

Like a birthmark: Coral understands, in her child's fashion, the power given to a priest, which he must carry with him

giggled suddenly like a child: increasingly, as he drinks, the priest will giggle; like a child he will try to forget the seriousness of his dilemma

the Morse code: for Coral, helping the priest is a game

something worse off than themselves: in the severely impoverished village—no food, no money—the priest is still the most abject

impatiently: the priest is not anxious to perform his duties

It is only polite to the father ... He is a very holy man: ironic, as the priest only wants to sleep

---

Part I, Chapter 4: The Bystanders

Among the 'bystanders', who observe the conflict between the priest and the lieutenant, is Mr Tench. On an impulse he decides to write a letter to his wife in England, whom he has not seen for many years. Padre José, another 'bystander', accidentally sees a burial in the cemetery, but refuses to say a prayer, because he is afraid of the authorities. When Luis's mother continues reading the story of Juan the Martyr, the boy reacts violently to the sentimentality and looks hopefully towards the soldiers marching by. When Mrs Fellows stops reading a history lesson, Coral goes to take charge of loading the bananas, a task her father has forgotten. The Chief of Police, suffering from a toothache, tells the lieutenant that he has permission to carry out his plan for catching the last priest—taking hostages from the villages, who will be shot if the village fails to report on the priest. On his way to the police station, the lieutenant shows Luis his gun and thinks of how he would remake the world for Mexican children.

NOTES AND GLOSSARY:

an odd impulse: has Mr Tench, in deciding to write to his wife, perhaps been touched by the power of God that the priest carries?

A memory stirred: Mr Tench will regularly remember the priest and will be a witness to his death

Con amistad: (*Spanish*) in friendship

there were no children about: ironically Padre José goes to the cemetery to be alone, but finds the funeral of a five-year-old girl

they hadn't been used to what the rest of the world knows best of all, the hope which peters out: for Catholics, in opposition to 'the rest of the world', hope has endured, in spite of the death of innocent children

a whole seducing choir of angels: ironically, in his cowardice, José sees the chance of performing a good action as a temptation, a seduction

for the flesh cannot always be strong: Greene satirises the conventional pieties of the story of Juan

Nobody could be such a fool: Luis understands the falseness of the story of Juan

sala: (*Spanish*) sitting-room

a place where you could sit out of this heat: Greene wrote in *The Lawless Roads*: 'Nothing in a tropical town can fill the place of a church for the most mundane use; a church is the one spot of coolness out of the vertical sun, a place to sit'*

Villa, Obregon, Madero, Huerta, Carranza: Mexican political figures of the era of the revolution. Villa, Obregon and Madero were assassinated

And so Lord Palmerston said: Mrs Fellows, reading Coral her history lesson, forms a parallel to Luis's mother. Both women are imparting useless information to children conscious of the real horrors of Mexican life

She carried her responsibilities carefully like crockery: another typical Greene comparison of the abstract and the concrete

The Lawless Roads, p.143.

as the mind grows up to the loss of tenderness: a typical expression of
Greene's vision of the horror of life

in her woman's pain: Coral is experiencing her first menstruation

big bold clever murals: the caricatured vices of the priesthood in the hall
of the Syndicate of Workers and Peasants include
two of the whisky priest's: desire for women and
drunkenness. Among the greatest of twentieth-
century Mexican artists were Rivera and Orozco,
whose murals of revolutionary themes Greene
discusses in *The Lawless Roads*

a sad and unsatisfiable love: the lieutenant, unlike the priest, Mr Tench
and Captain Fellows, has no child, but must try to
love Mexican children in the abstract, by giving
them a new society

the truth—a vacant universe: Greene emphasises the nihilism of the
lieutenant's view of life

a halo: ironically, the lieutenant's circling of the priest's
face in the photo suggests his saintliness

Part II, Chapter 1

The priest travelling through the countryside, trying to avoid the
soldiers, moves towards his old parish, Concepción, and the village
where he fathered a child, Brigitta, by Maria, one of his parishioners. He
is distressed at the cool welcome he receives, until he learns about the
policy of taking hostages. In the morning he says Mass just before the
police arrive. The lieutenant questions all the men and seems suspicious
of the priest, but does not recognise him. A hostage is taken, although
the priest, without identifying himself, volunteers to go in his place.
The villagers tell the priest he must go north to the next state but he
turns south towards Carmen, where he was born. He is searching for
wine for the Mass and hoping to be able to save Brigitta's soul. On his
way he is joined by a half-caste who has recognised him and hopes to
turn him in for reward. They spend the night in an abandoned hut. The
priest sleeps fitfully and thinks of his past career in a comfortable
parish. He tries to escape, but the half-caste joins him. Finally the
priest sends him on his own mule into Carmen and goes toward the
capital city.

NOTES AND GLOSSARY:

one more surrender: bit by bit the priest has lost all the outward
trappings of his vocation; but he carries on

He was a bad priest, he knew: this chapter is the first to be presented
from the priest's point of view

despair—the unforgivable sin: the priest echoes the thought of Padre José

It's not what you want or what I want: the priest feels, obscurely, that he is following the will of God

If he left they would be safe and they would be free from his example ... But it was from him too they took God—in their mouths: a clear statement of the priest's dilemma. Should he stay to say Mass, or leave, so that the people should not suffer for him, especially as he is a bad priest?

that small malicious child: Brigitta, the priest's illegitimate daughter, is another of the prematurely adult children produced by a society of suffering who play their parts in this novel

sacrificing an unimportant motion of the body: the priest, like the lieutenant, has known little of sexual desire

he had believed that when he was a priest he would be rich and proud: a confirmation of the lieutenant's idea of the priesthood. The whisky priest has, however, given up this youthful idea

messages with taps: the priest tries to interest his daughter in Coral's Morse code

Pain is part of joy: the necessity to experience pain is a crucial part of Greene's vision of life

Hoc est enim Corpus Meum: (*Latin*) 'This is my body'. The consecration of the bread, which becomes the body of Christ

a cock in the village crowed: perhaps an echo of the biblical scene when Christ says to Peter that he will betray him before the cock crows thrice. The priest, however, is not betrayed by the villagers

Instead of food they talk to you about heaven: the lieutenant's words put a different interpretation on the sermon the priest has just given

This child is worth more than the Pope in Rome: ironically it is the priest's daughter for whom the lieutenant also feels 'affection'. The priest later thinks 'this child was more important than a whole continent'. The lieutenant and the priest are fighting for Brigitta

I'm getting too old ... Take me: although he says 'It's my job not to be caught', the priest does not want to see an innocent man made hostage

You're no good any more to anyone: since Maria has destroyed the wine, the priest can no longer say Mass

There've been a lot of good thieves: an allusion to the good thief crucified next to Christ

The papers: as is apparent a few pages later, these are a few sheets of notes from the priest's former parish work

canines which stuck yellowly out: this man, a mestizo (half-caste of Indian and European blood), always identified by his two canine teeth, is the one who will betray the priest

he dreamed: the first of the priest's dreams is about his past, peaceful life, but becomes confused with an image of Montez, a hostage shot by the lieutenant

finca: (*Spanish*) estate, farm

pistolero: (*Spanish*) gangster

you talk like a priest: the first indication that the half-caste knows who the priest is

***Pater noster qui es in coelis*:** 'Our Father which art in heaven', the beginning of the Lord's Prayer in Latin

Judas: the half-caste will betray the priest, as Judas betrayed Christ

Prometheus: in Greek myth, Prometheus stole fire from the god Zeus and brought it to earth

he had said something about the Apostles: in the past the priest had jokingly compared himself to Christ; now, in his suffering he is closer to Christ

the local photographer: ironically the priest remembers when the photo was taken that is now being used by the lieutenant to try to identify him

a charming story: in the past the priest told sentimental stories like those Luis's mother reads

Perhaps Padre José was the better man: seeing pride and ambition in his own past, the priest now has the humility to compare himself unfavourably to Padre José. Later he thinks he is no more 'worthy' than the half-caste

the sin by which the angels fell: Lucifer revolted against God through pride and fell to hell

'You are a father, aren't you?' 'I have a child': the priest cleverly avoids a direct lie to the half-caste

of which he was only a typical part: the priest thinks of the similarity of all men's sins, echoing Greene's pessimism about human nature

his pride and lust and cowardice: once again the priest humbles himself

If that were goodness: the priest begins to react against the pieties of the conventionally good women of his parish, a theme that will be significant in the following chapters

He had given way to despair—and out of that had emerged a human soul and love—not the best love, but love all the same: the priest thinks of the despairing sexual act with Maria, and the birth of Brigitta, but his thought can also be seen as applying to his present situation. He grows in love, even for the half-caste, in the midst of his own despair

No Man's Land: the area between the opposing trenches during the First World War

God's image: the priest sees God not only in man's soul but, surprisingly, in his body, even in his sins: 'something resembling God . . . went into odd attitudes before the bullets in a prison yard or contorted itself like a camel in the attitude of sex': the priest's images include a prophesy of his own death as well as a memory from his past

only one place: the priest realises he must go to the city, but for that will need again to swap his clothes

---

Part II, Chapter 2

Having found a drill suit, the priest goes to the capital city, where a beggar promises to help him find some wine. They go to a hotel to buy confiscated wine and brandy from the Governor's cousin. In order not to create suspicion, he must offer the cousin and the beggar drinks. The Chief of Police arrives and drinks with them. When the wine is finished, the priest, who needed it for the Mass, begins to cry. He takes the remaining brandy with him and is chased by the Red Shirts and the Police. After trying to get Padre José to hide him, he is caught and put into prison for possessing alcohol.

NOTES AND GLOSSARY:

It was like a religious ceremony which had lost all meaning: in *The Lawless Roads*, Greene used the same phrase to describe Sunday evening promenades in Villahermosa*

The man in the shabby drill suit: Greene indicates that the priest has found different clothes. This chapter is initially narrated from outside, and the priest is not identified

---

The Lawless Roads, p.129.

as if he were considering a point of academic interest: the priest has not lost all his seminary training

fifteen pesos seventy-five centavos: approximately four U.S. dollars or a little less than two pounds sterling

their eyes met: the half-caste has seen the priest, an additional reason for him to get his communion wine and leave as quickly as possible

a voice said: as the lights are out, the narrative presents only the sounds. This is part of Greene's technique of cinematic realism in this scene, where everything is presented without explanation, as if by the camera's eye

I know how to keep a secret: ironically, the priest refers not to illicit dealings but to the secrets of the confessional

with a look of painful anxiety: the dark humour of this scene results from the unstated fact that the priest wants the wine for the Mass, but must pretend he only wants to drink

How is your toothache?: throughout the novel, the Chief of Police has a toothache, just as the priest always giggles

Salud: (*Spanish*) a toast, 'to your health'

life has such irony: speaking of a priest who was shot, the Chief of Police is, by an irony of which he is unaware, speaking to the last priest, and drinking the last of his communion wine

all the hope of the world draining away: the priest means, literally, that the hope of salvation, through the blood of Christ, has been drained away as the wine is finished

He can't be doing any good: ironically the priest can no longer do good, since the Chief of Police has finished the wine

Your face somehow: vaguely the Chief of Police remembers the photograph: a moment of suspense

words like 'mystery' and 'soul' and 'the source of life': only drunken conversation to the others, but to the priest full of bitter meaning, as the wine is gone

the priest: after the drinking scene, the priest is again identified in his true character

frontón: (*Spanish*) pelota court, for a game played with a hard ball and basket scoops, originating in the Basque country and popular in Mexico

the amateurs and the professionals: the young Red Shirts in the billiard parlour are having a game chasing the priest; to the police it is serious business.

like a guardian spirit: ironic, as José's wife represents the antithesis of a Christian guardian spirit

a little ball of paper: the priest has been carrying his parish notes with him until now

That was the fallacy of the death-bed repentance: in an earlier novel, *Brighton Rock*, Greene considers the possibility of a last-minute repentance for a life of crime. Here he suggests that such repentance is unlikely

it was as if he were under the influence of some secret passion: ironically, the lieutenant is preoccupied with catching the priest and so does not look at the man in front of him, who he thinks is only a smuggler

Hombre: (*Spanish*) man

have you never been in jail before?: the sergeant, who thinks he is dealing with a petty criminal, ironically predicts the significance of the priest's one night in jail

---

Part II, Chapter 3

The priest spends the night in prison, surrounded by criminals and victims of society. He comes to see this prison as the world in miniature, containing all the vices and virtues of which men are capable; he learns more compassion and humility. He speaks to a murderer, and sits next to an old man longing to see his illegitimate daughter, taken away from him by the Church. He argues with a pious woman, trying to destroy her 'sentimental notions of what is good'. Although he identifies himself, he is not betrayed by any of the prisoners in the morning. While he is cleaning the cells, he sees the half-caste, who decides not to turn him in immediately as he might not get the reward. While querying the priest, the lieutenant cannot remember where he saw him before. Feeling sorry for what he thinks to be a poor man, the lieutenant gives the priest five pesos.

NOTES AND GLOSSARY:

pleasure was going on: a couple making love in the dark, crowded prison are judged in various fashions by the other prisoners

you talk like a priest: the priest still makes his normal abstract moral judgements; 'It's a terrible thing to kill a man'

'bastard': the priest thinks of Brigitta, whom he loves as the old man loves his illegitimate daughter. The priest is now on the side of the old man, not of the Church officials who took his daughter away from him

This place was very like the world: overcrowded with lust and crime and unhappy love, it stank to heaven: the prison is the world in miniature, which also 'stinks to heaven'. 'Heaven', however, is God who will save man from the stink

Toothache is worse: a humorous echo of the problems of the Chief of Police

and the Governor up there in the square undoubtedly existed: the priest creates a parable, to explain that being brave because one does not believe in God will be pointless when, after death, one learns that God exists after all

The priest giggled: even in his fear, the priest is not quite serious

the sin seemed to him now so unimportant and he loved the fruit of it: the essence of the dilemma of *The Power and the Glory*. Love of Brigitta, the novel often implies, is a truly religious experience, giving the priest a worth transcending his actions, that are officially considered 'sins' by the Church

He was just one criminal among a herd of criminals: the priest realises his bond with all men

when pious people came kissing his black cotton glove: kissing the priest's glove is an action evoked several times to signify his past, easy life

it was my kind who robbed him: the priest rejects the official Church's condemnation of the old man

I know—from experience—how much beauty Satan carried down with him when he fell: the priest deliberately tries to shock the pious woman. Refusal strongly to condemn sexual sins is an attitude frequently present in Greene's work

he began to dream: the priest dreams of searching to save his daughter and forgetting the 'password'

a sign: the priest has faith that if he escapes this time, it will be God's will that he should leave Tabasco

He had obtained it at great risk: information about how the priest got his drill suit, given after the suit has been mentioned many times. One of Greene's techniques is to introduce bits of information at odd moments, to add to the suspense and uncertainty

He was begging: the pious woman has no mercy for the priest, but she does help him to deceive the sergeant

two fangs protruded: again the typical detail by which the reader knows the half-caste is in the cell

Advise me: ironically, the half-caste asks the priest when to turn him in for the reward. The priest, honestly, says 'they'd give you *something* even here'

God had decided: another moment of suspense has passed, the priest has not yet been betrayed. But the suspense begins again when he sees the lieutenant

it sometimes seemed to him that venial sins ... cut you off from grace more completely than the worst sins of all: in his misery the priest has learned love. Greene has often shown more sympathy for those who have committed mortal sins than for those, like the pious woman, who commit small sins of pride

God knows: the priest means this literally and the lieutenant takes it literally, although on the surface it seems merely a conventional expression of uncertainty

You're a good man: the lieutenant is morally good in ways which the priest is not

---

Part II, Chapter 4

The priest makes his way to the Fellows's bungalow, hoping that Coral can help him. He finds it deserted except for a wounded and famished mongrel bitch. Having had nothing to eat for two days the priest fights with the bitch for the remains of meat on a bone. Then he reads a book of English poetry that belonged to Coral. Later, he makes his way north and stops in an abandoned hut to avoid the rain. He discovers and tries to help a dying Indian child, who has been shot during a battle between James Calver and the soldiers. When the child dies, he goes with the mother to leave the body at the foot of a rough cross on the mountain. Increasingly feverish, he wanders on, seeing no life except for a few monkeys. He feels sure he will die. A man who approaches tells him he has come to a village with a church, in the next state.

NOTES AND GLOSSARY:

the flagstaff: a detail to make us aware that the priest has come to the Fellows's bungalow

a wounded or a broken leg: the appearance of the wounded bitch means that the bungalow is deserted, but also suggests some violence has taken place. The mystery of Coral's disappearance is only partially resolved, late in the novel

a pile of old medicine bottles ... only her mother: Mrs Fellows was a hypochondriac, continually taking medicine. The priest's relief to find that the medicine was hers shows the depth of his attachment to Coral

the American War of Independence: the priest finds some of Coral's notes from her correspondence school

her life had no importance beside that of a human being: for once the priest has no moral problems in trying to preserve his own life rather than the mongrel's

Virtus Laudata Crescit: (*Latin*) 'Excellence thrives on praises'

Come back! . . . my daughter: part of 'Lord Ullin's Daughter', by the Scottish poet, T. Campbell (1777–1844), which conveys to the priest his love for his own daughter

limbo: the border of Hell where the souls are gathered of those with no actual sin, but whose original sin was not washed away by baptism

Somebody: the priest feels God has willed that he meet no one. (Literally, as the reader learns gradually, it is the fight of the police with Calver that has forced all the people to flee)

you could never tell with Indians: the priest presumably is of European descent. The lieutenant, however, has 'Indian-blooded hands'

like flight, from force or disease: a detail, like the wounded bitch, suggesting some violence in the area

as if man . . . had been left to man: the violence makes it seem 'as if' God has abandoned the state

Americano: (*Spanish*) James Calver, the American bandit

the name of the banana station: the priest realises something happened at the Fellows's house, but cannot imagine Coral is dead

Iglesia: (*Spanish*) 'church'

the size of a baby's skull: the image to describe the lumps of sugar links their shared task of carrying the dead child to its burial place. In *The Lawless Roads* Greene describes being given a lump of sugar 'the size of a doll's head'.* The image has been changed to reinforce the meaning of the scene

A grove of crosses: Greene saw roughly hewn crosses made by Indians in the mountains while travelling to Las Casas: 'This was the Indian religion—a dark, tormented, magic cult'†

in a curious and complicated pattern: the Indian woman's Catholicism has been mixed with earlier, pagan beliefs. Greene describes seeing this pattern in Las Casas**

The Lawless Roads, p.194.
†*The Lawless Roads*, p.204.
**The Lawless Roads*, p.216.

Vamos: (*Spanish*) 'let's go'

as if they were brothers: the priest senses his link to James Calver: a premonition of the end of the novel

barranca: (*Spanish*) gully

O God, I have loved the beauty of Thy house: the priest's recitation (of Psalm 26:8) is ironic, as the natural world around him is so desolate

there were going to be no more hostages: at the moment when the priest has accepted his fate and lost all his pride, he has crossed the border and is safe

home: the walls of the church

Part III, Chapter 1

The priest stays with Mr Lehr and his spinster sister, Germans who had settled in the United States and then come to Mexico to farm. He soon feels like a deserter in their peaceful, well-ordered household. Although the church has been closed, and Mass is illegal, he is only liable to a fine in this state. He celebrates Mass, baptises children, hears confessions and feels his old habits returning. He even buys some brandy. The morning he is to leave for the city of Las Casas, where he will find priests and a chance to confess his sins, the half-caste arrives with a note from James Calver who is dying. Although he knows it is a trap, the priest returns across the border to hear Calver's confession. He rejects the possibility of peace.

NOTES AND GLOSSARY:

darning socks: an activity that immediately contrasts the scene with the rest of the novel, where most people have no shoes

Villa's men: Pancho Villa (1878–1923), a guerrilla leader and revolutionary

Too much luxury: Mr Lehr's criticism of the Church echoes the lieutenant's. To the priest after his experiences, it is hard to remember why such criticism could be made

the badge of a deserter: a premonition that the priest will not accept a peaceful life

Prison for a week: Catholicism is officially outlawed in this stage (Chiapas), but the persecution seems mild to the priest

the Gideons: an American organisation, founded in 1899, to spread Christianity by placing Bibles in hotel rooms for commercial travellers

over-simple explanations: after what the priest has experienced, the simple pieties of the Gideons' suggestions for biblical readings seem absurd

You don't like people to read the Bible: a common Protestant criticism of Catholicism

The schoolmaster: Greene wrote, in *The Lawless Roads*, of meeting a schoolmaster in Palengue, the only villager who was not a Catholic. 'Like all the school teachers now, he was a politician'*

God might forgive cowardice and passion, but was it possible to forgive the habit of piety?: a repetition of the priest's thoughts in the prison cell, but now he sees himself slipping back into his old habits

He drank the brandy down like damnation: another typical Greene simile, comparing the concrete to the abstract

only one peso for the baptisms: tempted by the chance to buy brandy, the priest decides to allow himself less money

Police News: the type of magazine devoted to stories of sexual misbehaviour and violence. Greene mocks Miss Lehr's spinsterish prudery. It is of interest, however, that she too feels a need to 'confess' to the priest

love should be happy and open: the priest always thinks of his love for Brigitta

odd sense of homesickness: the priest is at home only among those who have suffered in the state of Tabasco

Domine, non sum dignus: (*Latin*) 'Lord, I am not worthy'

What was the good of confession when you loved the result of your crime?: a central paradox of the novel, for the priest has grown in compassion through his sin

that woman in prison may have been the best person there: the priest realises he should not judge the pious too harshly. The tone of the novel, however, leads the reader to judge the pious more severely than the sinners

grease-proof paper: Miss Lehr's neatness contrasts to the greasy paper used to wrap food on which Calver wrote his message

The Prince of Denmark: the paper is part of Coral's school essay on Hamlet's famous soliloquy (in Shakespeare's *Hamlet*) 'To be or not to be'. Hamlet's dilemma corresponds to the priest's. Should he go towards Las Casas and live, or return with the half-caste to fulfil his duty as a priest?

The Lawless Roads, p.180.

For Christ's sake, father: James Calver's phrase can be read as profanity or as an appeal for the sake of Christ

a child to act as a screen: an explanation of why the Indian child died

It was only an Indian: a reflection of the racism of Mexican society

Conscience money?: the schoolmaster, who disapproves of religion, thinks the priest feels guilty for the money he has made. The priest, however, feels obscurely guilty for having even dreamed of a peaceful life

---

Part III, Chapter 2

After a seven-hour journey, the priest and the half-caste reach the hut where Calver is dying. The priest sends the mules back to the Lehrs and, after drinking some of his brandy, goes in to see Calver. Calver can only repeat that the priest must leave, saying he didn't understand what was happening. He does not confess his sins and dies while looking for a knife to give the priest for defence. The priest prays to God to forgive Calver, who was trying to help him.

NOTES AND GLOSSARY:

you-know-what: the priest needs brandy to face his ordeal

shocking bad luck . . . to be burdened with a sin of such magnitude: the priest no longer thinks of himself, but pities the half-caste

They? they?: the half-caste falls into the priest's trap and admits that the police are waiting

a voice said, 'Father': an echo of Judas's betrayal of Christ. See the Bible, Mark 14:45 'And as soon as he was come, he goeth straightway to him, and saith, Master, master', a signal for the soldiers to arrest Christ

Beat it: Calver, in a moment of nobility, tries to save the priest

Like the thief: a reference to the thief crucified with Christ, who repented at the last moment

children perhaps: the priest knows about the Indian child, but not about Coral, for whose death Calver is also responsible

whichever way you looked, there wasn't much merit in either of them: because of his sins the priest sees himself as only another criminal like Calver. To the lieutenant, of course, the priest, because of his religion, is the worse criminal

Part III, Chapter 3

After Calver dies, the lieutenant enters the hut to arrest the priest. The two talk together for the first time, each defending his position. After the rains stop the priest promises the half-caste to pray for him. Then they begin their march back to the capital. At night they again discuss their views of life. As they ride into the capital they are watched by Luis, who asks the lieutenant eagerly if the priest has been captured.

NOTES AND GLOSSARY:

badly-affected ease: the priest is terrified, but tries to appear calm

They looked two of a kind, dirty and unshaved: the lieutenant seemed to belong to a different class: again the contrast between the neat, well-behaved lieutenant and the shabby priest, who is more like Calver

He did no real harm: the lieutenant does not see Calver as a social menace

a pack of cards: throughout, the priest has wanted to show card tricks to children. Now his audience is the least child-like person he has met, the lieutenant

a good man: the priest can see the moral qualities of the lieutenant, who for his part says, 'I have nothing against you ... as a man'. The conflict is between their ideas

Today is Sunday: the priest begins his procession to the capital on Sunday, an echo of Palm Sunday, when Christ entered Jerusalem before his Crucifixion

Does the jefe feel like that too?: the priest of course has met the Chief of Police, though he does not tell the lieutenant of that encounter

the world's unhappy whether you are rich or poor: changing the economic structure of society will, for the priest, make no difference to the corruption and suffering of mankind

there won't always be good men in your party: the essence of the priest's argument is that good men are not necessary to the Church, since even a bad priest can give the sacraments

He gets caught up: the only time the priest tries to explain why he stayed in Tabasco he has no clear reason to offer

just as it did at school when a bully I had been afraid of: in many of Greene's novels characters remember the unhappiness of their school days, an echo of Greene's own childhood

pride was at work: the priest blames his sins on pride. It is one vice he has now completely lost

Go . . . you've done your job: an echo of the Roman soldiers dismissing Judas: 'And they said, What is that to us?' (See the Bible, Matthew 27:4)

I'll pray for you: the priest's willingness to pray for the half-caste is an echo of Christ's words on the cross: 'Father, forgive them; for they know not what they do' (See the Bible, Luke 23:34). The priest, with his knowledge, 'expected nothing else of anything human' than what the half-caste has done

'I wanted to give them the whole world' . . . 'Perhaps that's what you did': the hostages, dying for their faith, may, from the priest's perspective, have gained the world of eternity

It's better to let him die in dirt and wake in heaven: from the priest's point of view, life on earth is of minor importance; what counts is the salvation of the soul

And a girl puts her head under water: the priest's argument against human love, that it causes suffering, echoes an experience of Greene's own youth, when a pregnant girl in his town committed suicide. The story is told in *The Lawless Roads*

if there's ever been a single man in this state damned, then I'll be damned too: the priest's feeling of responsibility for others echoes that of Charles Péguy (1873– 1914), a French Catholic writer who wanted to be damned if any other men were damned, and refused the sacraments. Greene refers to him in the Prologue to *The Lawless Roads*: 'Péguy challenging God in the cause of the damned'*

It wasn't a very triumphal procession: an ironic allusion to Christ's entrance into Jerusalem on Palm Sunday

If there's anything I can do for you: the lieutenant again shows kindness

No pulse, no breath, no heart-beat, but it's still life—we've only got to find a name for it: the lieutenant needs a scientific explanation for what the priest has described as the miracle of those who seem dead but then come back to life

A small boy: Luis re-enters the story, watching the lieutenant bring the priest in. The battle for Luis's soul will form the final drama of the novel

*The Lawless Roads, p.3.

Part III, Chapter 4

Having promised the priest that he would ask Padre José to give confession, the lieutenant goes after dark to José's house. José would like to go, but his wife, frightened of possible persecution or loss of their pension, refuses to allow him to perform his duty as a priest. The whisky priest feels completely abandoned and the lieutenant, after giving him an illegal flask of brandy, leaves the cell feeling suddenly empty, without purpose. The priest tries to confess his sins, but keeps thinking of his daughter and praying for her salvation. He is frightened and even thinks of offering to get married to save his life. Then he has another strange dream, in which Coral brings him wine and 'news'. He wakes at dawn before his execution, confused and only aware how useless his life has been.

NOTES AND GLOSSARY:

one didn't trust one's superiors: the lieutenant, more doctrinaire than the Chief of Police, is nevertheless willing to disobey the law for the priest

If it's anything about a burial: Padre José is afraid, even though he refused to say a prayer for the dead child (Part I, Chapter 4)

perhaps she lived in bed: Padre José's wife's sexual appetites are mocked several times in the novel

and the pension will be stopped: Padre José's wife, acting from self-interest, contrasts with the lieutenant

the general laughter . . . chiming up all round: the image of the laughter of the children chiming like church bells completes the humiliation of Padre José

Sometimes I feel you're just trying to talk me round: the priest has sown doubts in the lieutenant's mind. As he leaves the cell he feels 'without a purpose'

a long passage in which he could find no door: the lieutenant's dream echoes the priest's dream of knocking on a door that would not open (Part II, Chapter 3). For the lieutenant there is no door to eternity

As the liquid touched his tongue he remembered his child: his two sins are connected in his mind

even a dentist: Mr Tench reappears in the priest's thoughts, just prior to the execution Mr Tench will witness

the best dish of all: the body and blood of Christ

the child at the banana station: suddenly in his dream Coral is bringing salvation, wine and then a signal in Morse referring to 'news', perhaps the 'good news' of the Gospel

disappointment because he had to go to God empty-handed: Is the priest, with no pride left, perhaps closer to saintliness than he realises?

He knew now that at the end there was only one thing that counted—to be a saint: the final sentence of Part III is translated from *Le Désespéré* (1887) by the French writer Léon Bloy (1846–1917)

Part IV

Captain and Mrs Fellows are in the capital city preparing to return to England and carefully avoiding speaking of Coral's death. There is excitement in the town because it is the morning of the priest's execution. Mr Tench is attending to the Chief of Police's bad tooth, neglected for months; but his hand is jumpy because he is suffering from indigestion. Just as he finishes drilling the tooth, he hears the noise of the preparation for the execution, which he watches from the window. Sickened, he decides to leave Mexico. Luis's mother reads the end of the story of Juan the Martyr, who died with great heroism, and then proclaims that the whisky priest is also a martyr. Luis, proud to have known a hero, spits with disgust on the lieutenant's gun as he passes in the street. Later, hearing a knock on the door, Luis opens it to find a new priest who has just arrived in Tabasco.

NOTES AND GLOSSARY:

She felt that she had been prematurely buried: Mrs Fellows is always hypochrondiac, afraid of death, but in an abstract, self-pitying way that contrasts with the real fears of the priest which immediately precede Part IV

We've got our own life to lead: Mrs Fellows wants to shut out all thoughts of Coral. This is the first clear indication that Coral is dead

an odd effect of being children: Coral had more sense of responsibility than her parents

There are so many priests: Mrs Fellows is not even aware of what has been happening in Mexico

A cookanheat: a stove for cooking and warming the house. The banality of Mrs Fellows's desires contrasts with the tragic grandeur of the drama going on around her, of which she is quite unaware

It wasn't my fault. If you'd been home: Mrs Fellows refuses to accept any responsibility

the way she went on afterwards: was Coral touched by grace through the priest?

I've never seen a mouth as bad as yours—except once: ironically, Mr Tench thinks of the priest, just prior to the execution

Seems she has got religion of some kind: has Mr Tench's wife been touched by grace, perhaps as a result of the priest? (Ironically, however, Greene indicates that the religion is not Catholic, as she offers her husband a divorce)

he was doing his best—it was only that his legs were not fully under his control: the priest's final moments, as observed by Mr Tench, show his attempt at dignity, his fear, and perhaps the effect of the brandy

one ought to do something: vague and ineffectual as ever, Mr Tench would like to help

the officer stuffing his gun back into his holster: the text suggests that the lieutenant, out of mercy, fired a single shot to end the priest's suffering when he was not dead after the volley of rifle shots

in the last chapter things always happened violently: with irony Greene comments on his own novel as well as on the story of Juan the Martyr

He was quite calm and happy: the death of the priest contrasts ironically with the sentimentality of the pious story

coup de grâce: (*French*) 'finishing stroke'

Saul the persecutor: Saul of Tarsus, who persecuted the Christians, received God's grace and became Paul, the greatest missionary of the early Church and the author of several epistles in the New Testament

He may be one of the saints: Luis's mother has changed her opinion of the whisky priest, now that he has been shot. She even invents a heroic death for him

the dynamic love . . . felt flat and dead: as the priest predicted, the lieutenant finds human love insufficient

He dreamed: Luis too has a dream, in which he sees reality rather than his mother's pieties

before the other could give himself a name: the new priest, 'with a rather sour mouth', is nameless as was the whisky priest. It is the function, not the individual, that matters

Part 3

Commentary

The title, *The Power and the Glory*

The title of the novel comes from the final words of the Lord's Prayer, 'for thine is the kingdom and the power and the glory'. The power and the glory are God's. The initial effect of the title, given the squalid Mexican atmosphere Greene portrays, is ironic. There seems to be no power or glory in a Church reduced to Padre José and the whisky priest. At the conclusion, however, the whole novel takes on another colouring and the sordid sequence of events may be seen as part of a divine plan through which God's power and glory are manifested in the weakest of men.

The characters

The priest and the lieutenant

The two principal characters, neither of them given a name, are present-ed through a series of parallels and contrasts, so that the reader is contin-ually invited to compare them, and to see an essential theme of the novel through this comparison: faith is more essential than a moral life. The priest is not virtuous, but his faith in God enables him finally to triumph over the lieutenant, a morally good man with no religious faith.

The priest had a calm childhood, and early decided to join the priest-hood in order to be admired and respected and to lead an enjoyable life. The lieutenant had a hard, poverty-stricken childhood in a part-Indian family; seeing that the Church took money from the poor and seemed to support the respectable middle classes, he decided to join the revolutionaries. The lieutenant, in contrast to the priest, began with dedication to a principle.

The lieutenant, lean and strong, lives a pure, ascetic life, is neat, without vices and without interest in women. The priest, by contrast, was fat and flabby, enjoying good food and eventually became an alcoholic. While not strongly interested in women, he fathered a child. Since becoming an outlaw, he is shabby and disreputable. The lieuten-ant is serious. The priest giggles often, and enjoys playing card tricks.

It is the lieutenant, however, who feels empty and without purpose when the novel ends. He has placed all his faith in building a new revolutionary society, towards which the first step is the elimination of all priests. Once he has accomplished this task, he has no concrete goals, nor does he have an attachment to any individual person. His faith is abstract. The priest, on the other hand, although his life has been sinful and although he was often motivated by pride rather than love of God, has grown in stature through his sins and his suffering. His pride is completely destroyed; he sees himself as only a common criminal, no better than those in prison, comparable to James Calver. He has learned as well the power of love, through his love for his daughter, Brigitta, for whom he is willing to sacrifice not only his life but his soul. The lieutenant is moved by anger, the priest by pity and love.

The conflict between the two men could be seen in terms of a fight for Brigitta: the typical poor village child who must be saved from superstition and given a better material life, according to the lieutenant; his daughter, whom he loves more than his own soul, to the priest.

There is a sense in which the priest and the lieutenant are alike, in contrast to most of the characters in the novel. Both are aware that the meaning of life is more than seeking for daily comforts. The lieutenant with faith in the revolution (although he also believes that the universe is dying and meaningless), the priest with faith in God's mercy, are far removed from Padre José's wife's worries about her pension, Mrs Fellows's desire for a 'cookanheat', or Luis's mother's search for holy relics.

Secondary characters

The secondary characters are usually developed in only a few short scenes. They often function to illustrate themes, or to bring out the central conflict of the priest and the lieutenant through parallels and contrasts. These characters represent various degrees of belief and various degrees of corruption. One critic has suggested that the characters in Graham Greene's novels can be divided into: the pious, the sinners, the innocents and the humanists.*

The pious, those whose religion is smug and self-satisfied, who feel little sense of sin, are mainly the objects of satire: Luis's mother and his little sisters, the pious woman in prison. Miss Lehr is similar, yet treated with more sympathy, because she is kind to the priest. Since she

*Laurence Lerner, 'Graham Greene', *Critical Quarterly*, V (1963), reprinted in R.W.B. Lewis and Peter J. Conn, editors, *The Power and the Glory*, The Viking Press, New York, 1970, p.400.

is not a Catholic, she is outside the realm in which God could speak to her and make her aware of real sin.

In Greene's world the sinners are, therefore, Catholic. Some are minor sinners, again treated mostly as objects of satire, such as José's wife, who is only interested in sex and her pension. Even the Chief of Police seems mostly an ineffectual man, unaware of the enormity of what he is condoning. Real sinners, objects of interest in Greene's world because they are closer to God, are Padre José, the nameless half-caste, James Calver, and the whisky priest himself. Padre José, old, fat, desolate, is an object of scorn because of his weakness in refusing to say a prayer at the child's burial and in refusing to hear the whisky priest's confession. His background explains to some extent his weakness. He was insecure in the pre-revolutionary Church and looked down upon as unintelligent. He has at least the virtue of humility. Even in his confidence in his damnation he remains close to God. The nameless half-caste is thoroughly despicable (but the priest in his charity understands the lengths to which poverty may push a man). The possibility of grace, however slight, remains nonetheless, as it does for James Calver, the American bandit who wanted to make a death-bed confession, but instead tries to help the priest. Calver at least follows his own code of honour among criminals.

The innocents among the characters are not children, but Captain and Mrs Fellows. Although they pretend to a vague belief in God, they are basically childlike in their incomprehension. Captain Fellows lives on the surface of life, happy to do a 'man's work', by which he means simple, physical labour. Mrs Fellows is sentimental, vague, hypochondriac; without intentionally causing harm she is probably responsible for her daughter's death: 'It wasn't my fault', she says. The Lehrs, too, in their incomprehension of real evil, may be considered among the 'innocents'. Mr Lehr, in spite of pacifist principles in his youth, readily adapts to the corrupt Mexican society. He is filled with anti-Catholic prejudices. Mr Tench is also an innocent, incapable of perceiving the real reasons for his sense of desolation, blaming the devaluation of the peso, Mexican food that gives him indigestion, poor Japanese dental drills, for his inability to reach God. In Greene's world the innocents are non-Catholics.

The humanists, in Greene's novels, are those who rely on categories of right and wrong, rather than good and evil, who judge the effects of action only in the temporal world and who actively reject the divine. Often, as in the case of the lieutenant, they are more virtuous in their lives than are the believers.

There are also a few minor figures—Luis's father who carries on, accepting Padre José and the whisky priest as the only Church there is; Maria, the mother of the priest's child, fighting only for safety for herself and Brigitta—who illustrate the sense of social doom in Mexico and the apparent abandonment of humanity by God. The novel holds out no hope for the betterment of their society. That they are not abandoned by God is only implied at the end of the novel. Oddly, Maria is a slight figure. The priest feels no real affection for her. His love is centred on his child, Brigitta, and, strangely, on Coral Fellows.

The children

The children are not simple innocent souls, but are already influenced by the corruption and the decay of their world. Their personalities seem formed. A poem that Greene has often quoted, 'Germinal' by the Irish author A.E. (pen name of G.W. Russell, 1867–1935), concludes: 'In the lost boyhood of Judas/Christ was betrayed'. The children often seem to be the battleground for the opposing forces represented by the lieutenant and the priest. They may, however, already be beyond the lieutenant's influence. The priest, on the other hand, needs only to reach their souls, to open them to the possibility of grace. And he, unlike the lieutenant, sees them as individuals, not a collective 'children of Mexico'.

Luis is presented simply, in his reactions to the pious story his mother reads and in his childish attraction to violence. If he chooses finally the priest's side, it seems to be for the wrong reason—a desire to have known a real hero. Only from a religious, not a psychological perspective, can his conversion be seen as a victory.

Brigitta, for whom the priest would sacrifice his soul, is the toughest, least admirable of the children. At the age of six, it is implied, she has already been badly touched by the world's corruption. Yet, given the strange perspective of God's mercy implied throughout the novel, the reader cannot judge Brigitta's soul.

Coral is the most interesting of the children, because she both shoulders adult responsibilities and loves childish games. She seems in attitudes and emotions the closest of any of the characters to the whisky priest. The strange attachment the priest feels for her gives her such prominence in the novel; otherwise she is only briefly presented.

The themes

Religious themes

Greene has said that the theme of his trilogy of religious novels— *Brighton Rock*, *The Power and the Glory* and *The Heart of the Matter* —is embodied in a phrase spoken by the priest in *Brighton Rock*:

'You can't conceive the appalling strangeness of the mercy of God.'*

Greene's conception of the power of God, of the overwhelming significance of the sacraments of the Roman Catholic Church, and of the presence of grace in the temporal world, even in the midst of suffering, underlies *The Power and the Glory* and constitutes its essential theme.

The power of the priest

In 1957 Greene said that *The Power and the Glory* was 'an attempt to understand a permanent religious situation: the function of the priesthood. I was much more interested in the theological point of view than in the political one.'† The Catholic priest, when he is ordained, is given the power to turn wine and bread into the blood and body of Christ during the sacrament of the Mass. This power, once given, cannot be taken away. It matters not that the whisky priest has led a dissolute life, nor even that Padre José has renounced his vocation and married his housekeeper. Both men are still priests and still retain the powers given to them at ordination.

The mystery of grace

The world is God's and, in spite of the ugliness, suffering and depravity in which mankind lives, God is always present, moving in mysterious ways through the most banal events of daily life. The priest has been given an enormous power in bringing God to man in the Mass. To receive God through taking the body and blood of Christ is to give oneself an opportunity to benefit from his grace and be saved from eternal damnation.

This is why the priest feels he must carry on, must continue to bring the sacraments to the villagers. He has lost his social and institutional roles; the guilds, the processions now seem meaningless. He knows he is in no way an exemplary man, capable of offering others a model of Christian virtue. But he can still bring them 'God in the mouth'. When the priest says Mass in Brigitta's village 'He could hear the sigh of breaths released: God was here for the first time in six years'. Because of the significance of the Mass, the priest weeps bitterly when all the wine he has purchased from the Governor's cousin disappears. The primacy of the sacraments, suggested throughout the novel, also negates Mr Lehr's criticism of Catholicism for not encouraging reading of the Bible. Receiving the Mass is more essential.

*Interview with Gene D. Phillips, 'Graham Greene. On the Screen', *The Catholic World*, August 1969.
†Interview with Philip Toynbee, *The Observer*, 15 September 1957.

In *The Power and the Glory*, those who have come into contact with the priest, even without the benefit of the sacrament of communion, are changed. Greene only hints at these changes, never attributing them directly to divine intervention, and often offering alternative psychological explanations, so that they might seem explicable on purely human terms. To try to overcome his feeling of being abandoned and without purpose, Mr Tench decides suddenly to write to his estranged wife. This decision may have been motivated simply by his chance to talk about his family with the priest; presumably he seldom had occasion to speak English in Mexico (and his Spanish is very bad). Greene does not mention this possibility, nor does he say that Mr Tench was touched by grace; but the novel suggests that something inexplicable in human terms may have happened. Coral changed perceptibly after her encounter with the priest. Greene, however, avoiding any attempt to portray directly the effect of grace, does not show us much of this change, and even provides a natural explanation, as her encounter with the priest coincides with the onset of puberty. Similarly, Luis's rejection of the lieutenant could be seen simply as a child's desire to have known a hero. Even the arrival of the new priest in Tabasco may seem fortuitous. Taken all together, however, the incidents suggest the mysterious power of God's grace. Despite first appearances, Tabasco has not been abandoned. Ironically, it is the one human being whom the priest wants desperately to save, Brigitta, for whom the novel gives no suggestion that grace will descend. Avoiding any hint of sentimentality, Greene suggests that the ways of God are unfathomable and not related to such human desires as paternal love.

The supremacy of religious to secular power

Given a belief in the omnipotence and omnipresence of God, the salvation the priest offers is far superior to that of the lieutenant. There is no possibility of the kingdom on earth that the lieutenant would like to build. While the novel shows compassion for the poor and the suffering, the misery of life in Tabasco is presented not as a social problem that could be solved by political means but as the common condition of men. Mr Tench suffers because of the devaluation of the peso, but his desolation is fundamentally spiritual. The Fellows are not disturbed by the poverty of the region and even seem unaware of the political struggles, but their lives are unhappy. *The Power and the Glory* thus suggests that the lieutenant's dream of a 'new world' is false because it ignores both the floods and torrents of the natural world and the corruptible nature of man. The only kingdom is in God's eternity.

Human nature

Greene does not expect much of mankind: 'Human nature is not black and white but black and grey.'* In commenting on the novels of Ford Madox Ford (1873–1939), he wrote: 'The little virtue that existed only attracted evil. But to Mr Ford, a Catholic...this was neither surprising nor depressing'.† Greene often portrays those who would conventionally be regarded as sinners as being closer to God than those who lead upright, virtuous lives. He chose as an epigraph to *The Heart of the Matter* a quotation from Charles Péguy: 'The sinner is at the heart of Christianity'. The sinner is aware of the evil in the world. For Greene awareness of evil precedes awareness of good. In many of his novels the pious, such as the woman to whom the priest talks in prison, seem unable fully to understand life because they are unaware of their own sinful nature. The sinner, however, because he knows he is not good and the world is full of misery and corruption, is in a position to be touched by grace.

If he often seems to dwell on the weaknesses and cruelty of men, Greene is also aware of what is similar in every person, made in God's image. A religious sense is, he believes, necessary to a full understanding of man. Writing about the novelist Henry James (1843–1916) he said: 'with the death of James the religious sense was lost to the English novel, and with the religious sense went the sense of the importance of the human act'.** Men are often weak, corrupt, cruel, but they are made in God's image and thus have a worth that cannot be explained in terms of their moral virtues and vices or in terms of their social roles.

Social themes

Greene portrays the misery of the villagers whom the priest visits after leaving the Fellows's bungalow. Through the priest's memories he satirises a Church which seemed to ignore that misery, a Church in which 'an energetic priest was always known by his debts'. In *The Lawless Roads* Greene is openly critical of a Catholic Action meeting he attended in Texas, supposedly in support of poor workers. It was a miserable performance: 'Catholicism, one felt, had to rediscover the technique of revolution'. He wondered how the good Catholic ladies would have reacted to the words of St James: '(quoted by Pope Pius XI in one of his last encyclicals), "Go to now, ye rich men: weep and howl in your miseries which shall come upon you"... Those are the words

Collected Essays, p.18.
†*Collected Essays*, p.161.
**Collected Essays*, p.115.

of revolution'.* Writing in the 1930s in the midst of a world-wide depression, Greene was aware of the faults of the institutionalised Catholic Church, although he tends to think that the Pope was on the side of the poor. Some of this criticism is apparent as a minor theme in *The Power and the Glory*.

Structure and narrative technique

The book is divided into four parts. Part I may be considered an introduction to the pursuit of the priest, in which he is presented and commented upon in various ways by the minor characters: Mr Tench, Luis's mother, Padre José, the Fellows, and the poor villagers. The priest is seen from the outside in Part I and is absent from Part I, Chapter 4. The effect of Part I is thus to create a milieu in which the priest hardly exists as an individual. This technique points to a major theme: the priest is significant first of all in his function, not his personality.

Part II primarily recounts the priest's flight from the lieutenant. He goes to the village where Brigitta lives, then, learning about the taking of hostages, escapes to the city, where he is imprisoned for possession of brandy. Released, he struggles towards the border of Chiapas. With the exception of the drinking scene, in Part II events are presented from the priest's point of view.

Part III is the conclusion of the pursuit. The priest agrees to return to Tabasco, is captured and executed. Again the events are told from his point of view, with one exception, the scene in which the lieutenant goes to see Padre José.

Part IV, a single chapter, gives reactions to the priest's execution by many of the characters present in Part I: the Fellows, Mr Tench, the lieutenant, Luis. As in Part I, the personality of the priest is no longer as significant as his role in the community.

The Power and the Glory therefore begins and ends with the community, a representative cross-section of mankind, as it has been touched by the life and death of the priest. In the two central sections are presented, first the priest's flight to safety and then his return and death. At the centre of the novel (Part II, Chapter 3—the seventh of the thirteen chapters) is the scene of the priest's night in prison, which may be seen as his *epiphany*, the moment when truth is revealed to him and he loses all his pride. He identifies with the sins of mankind, represented by the inmates, which have been his sins as well— fornication, siring an illegitimate child, rigid piety, drunkenness. But, he also finds love; none of the sinners is willing to betray him for reward.

The Lawless Roads, p.21.

The events of the plot in the two central and longest parts are also carefully arranged as a suspense story, in which the priest is pursued both by the lieutenant and by God. The priest meets the lieutenant in the village (Part II, Chapter 1) and at the prison (Part II, Chapter 3), and both times is almost caught. In Part III, with the help of the half-caste, the lieutenant sets his trap and the priest is captured. Parallel to this pursuit and capture is the implied pursuit of the priest by God. Is it perhaps God's will that he is called to a sick bed and prevented from escaping on the boat and that he is not captured in the village, but goes into the city where he will endure prison? Then, when the priest thinks his release is a sign from God that he should leave Tabasco, he feels like a deserter at the Lehr's house. God has perhaps prepared him to accept his return and death. The structure emphasises both the priest's role within the community of souls seeking salvation and his pursuit by the law and by divine will.

Cinematic effects

Much of the force of *The Power and the Glory* comes from the artistry with which Greene has varied the point of view and placed scenes for effects of contrast and parallel. Scenes are juxtaposed as in montage in a film. (Montage is the technique by which the film director 'cuts' from one sequence to another, to suggest that two plot lines are occurring simultaneously, or to suggest a comparison or a contrast between characters or incidents.) In Part I, Chapter 2, Greene shifts abruptly from the lieutenant to Luis's mother, then to Padre José. Presumably all three incidents are occurring at the same time. A similar effect is achieved in Part I, Chapter 4 as the scene shifts from Mr Tench to Padre José to Luis to Coral to the lieutenant. Then, the following chapter, the first of Part II, recounts roughly the same period of time from the perspective of the priest.

As well as indicating simultaneity in time, the montage technique permits the author to establish implicit parallels. In Part I, Chapter 2, for example, the scene shifts suddenly from the lieutenant lying in his bed thinking of his hatred of religion, to Luis sitting on his bed, bored with his mother's story of Juan the Martyr. At this point the reader feels that Luis will join the lieutenant. After Luis's father says 'the Church is Padre José' the scene 'cuts' to the old, fat priest sitting on a packing-case, an implicit confirmation of the father's pessimism about 'the extent of their abandonment'. In Part I, Chapter 3 a social contrast is apparent in the juxtaposition of the comfort of the Fellows's bungalow and the abject poverty of the village; but there is also a contrast between the Fellows's lack of religion and the abiding faith of the poor. Part I, Chapter 4, a series of short scenes about the 'bystanders', implies comparisons, as each of them is concerned with problems of marriage and children. Luis's mother reads about Juan the Martyr, then the action shifts to Coral's mother reading a correspondence school history lesson. Both stories are irrelevant to the lives of the children. The lieutenant feels a sense of responsibility for the children of Mexico, in contrast to the cowardice of Padre José, the ineffectual efforts of Mr Tench to write to his own family, Luis's mother's inability to understand her son, and Mrs Fellows's abandonment of all responsibility to Coral. In Part IV there are again swift 'cuts' and implied comparisons. The scene with the Fellows 'fades out' abruptly when Mrs Fellows 'turned her head, swathed in handkerchief'. The next scene begins with Mr Tench speaking to the Chief of Police about his tooth. Two kinds of pain link the two scenes. After seeing the execution, Mr Tench thinks of his children. The following scene begins with Luis's mother reading to her children the story of the execution of Juan, which includes a 'Chief of Police'. This kind of montage, establishing parallels and contrasts by sudden shifts of scene, is most prevalent in the first and fourth parts of the novel, where Greene establishes the communal context of the priest's life and death. Part II, the flight, and Part III, the return, are narrated linearly.

Another cinematic technique used in *The Power and the Glory* is the 'pan shot', in which the camera moves across a scene from side to side, showing various details before settling on a significant feature. Greene, for example, begins the novel with such a 'shot' of the port, before focusing on Mr Tench. Similarly in Part II, Chapter 2, he presents an evening in the capital city, then 'brings the camera in' on 'the man in the drill suit'.

Greene occasionally also uses the 'flashback', when a scene from the past is inserted to comment upon or explain the motivation of a character. Without intervening directly as a narrator to explain a situation, he is thus able to give the reader sufficient information to understand the priest's development. There are two examples of this kind of flashback in *The Power and the Glory*. In Part II, Chapter 1, while riding a mule into Brigitta's village, the priest thinks of the past few years, when he gradually surrendered all the trappings of the priesthood; later in the same chapter, the priest looks at his old parish notes and remembers a dinner given in his honour. Greene does not often, however, explain the past; the priest exists primarily in his present suffering.

The novelist can, of course, more directly than the film director, show us the events from the point of view of one character, and give us this character's thoughts about what he is seeing. Greene varies the point of view, presenting each scene as it appears to one of the characters, with the exception of the scene of the purchase of the wine. In this scene, by describing the actions of 'the man in the drill suit' from the outside, Greene creates an ironic discrepancy between what occurs on the surface, as the 'camera eye' sees it, and the underlying meaning of the search for communion wine.

Time in the novel

Because of Greene's use of montage effects, although some clues are given, the reader is required to work out for himself how time passes between the various scenes. An outline of the time scheme follows:

I,1: Mr Tench meets the priest; the priest then goes to see the sick woman.

I,2: One week later, after hearing that the priest has been sighted, the lieutenant plans the policy of taking hostages. The other events in the chapter (involving Luis's mother and Padre José) happen at the same time.

I,3: About one month later, the priest arrives at the Fellows's home.

I.4: A week or two later, five events occur at roughly the same time, involving Mr Tench, Padre José, Luis's family, Coral, the lieutenant.

II,1: A few days after the events in I,4, the priest goes to Brigitta's village, meets the lieutenant for the first time, then continues his journey.

II,2: About a week later, the priest arrives in Villahermosa and is captured.

II,3: The same night, the priest is in prison.

II,4: A few days later, the priest flees towards the border.

III,1: A few days later, the priest is at the Lehr's house for several days, until the half-caste arrives.

III,2: The day the priest sees Calver, the same day he has left the Lehr's house.

III,3: The same day, the priest and the lieutenant talk.

III,4: A few days later, the priest awaits his execution.

IV: The following morning, several people react to the execution.

The action of *The Power and the Glory* thus takes place during a period of about nine or ten weeks, the last weeks of the priest's life. Part I covers the longest period of time. From Part II, Chapter 4 to the end of the novel events are told almost day by day, covering a period of about ten days. Between chapters, especially early in the novel, there are usually gaps in time, in which the reader does not know what has happened. Greene's method is to present blocks of time from the point of view of one character, with no narrator to fill in between the scenes. The reader does not know, for example, how the half-caste tracked the priest to the Lehr's house, or exactly what happened to Coral. Greene's treatment of time is similar to that of a film director who presents only images of particular moments. In a critical essay Greene said 'one begins to wonder whether any novelist has found it possible to express the passage of time directly'.* Greene's solution is not to attempt to show the passage of time, but to leave the gaps between dramatic incidents unfilled.

The parallels to the life of Christ

The story of the whisky priest often presents parallels to the life of Christ. Like Christ tempted by Satan in the wilderness, the priest going towards Chiapas faces the temptation of escape to avoid his destiny. Like Christ, however, he submits himself to what he considers the will of God. His return by mule to Tabasco recalls Christ's entry by mule into Jerusalem on the Sunday before the crucifixion. The priest is not, however, able to pray for his enemies at the moment of his death as did Christ. Instead his death has little dignity. While Christ stumbled under the heavy weight of the cross, the whisky priest's legs are not under his control, presumably the effect of fear or too much brandy. His life may recall Christ's, but he is too human, too weak.

The priest is surrounded by characters who in odd ways bring to mind biblical characters. Brigitta's mother, Maria, may bring to mind Mary Magdalene, a former prostitute who served Christ. The half-caste, a Catholic, one of the priest's own kind, like Judas betrays his master to the enemy for money. (Several direct echoes of the biblical story are mentioned in the notes to Part III, Chapters 2 and 3.) James Calver (the name recalls Calvary, the place where Christ was crucified) presents a parallel to Barabbas, a common criminal who was brought to justice at the same time as Christ. It was a custom for one criminal to be released during the feast of the Passover; the people demanded the release of Barabbas. (The lieutenant, who says that Calver did no real harm, has vowed to destroy the priest.) Calver is also a parallel to the good thief, who was crucified next to Christ, believed in him and repented. Christ said to this thief: 'Today shalt thou be with me in paradise' (Luke 23:43). This parallel is, however, ambiguous, since the question of whether Calver is saved or damned cannot be resolved. An analogy is implied between the lieutenant and the Romans responsible for the crucifixion. The Chief of Police, in the background, permitting the execution but not really desiring it, has similarities to Pontius Pilate. Ironically, however, it is Mr Tench rather than the Chief who washes his hands a moment before the priest is shot.

Greene seems to mock the parallel of the whisky priest to Christ,

Collected Essays, pp.72–3.

however, by suggesting a similar parallel when Padre José is tempted in the cemetery, thus making José as well an ironic Christ-figure. Many of the biblical parallels—such as Mr Tench washing his hands, or José's temptation—are deliberately ambiguous. When Luis's mother speaks of obtaining a relic, a piece of handkerchief soaked in the priest's blood, is the reader expected recall the Roman soldiers casting lots for Christ's clothing? In spite of her insipid piety, Luis's mother does not seem to present a parallel to a soldier crucifying Christ. Perhaps instead of looking for consistent parallels between characters and the story of Christ (which would suggest an allegory), we should regard the novel as an expression of Greene's personal vision, in which events in the present-day world are seen in connection with, as parallel to, or as inversions of, the Christian story.

Suspense thriller or divine pattern?

The Power and the Glory is told in a deliberately disjointed fashion, which serves both to create suspense and to suggest that behind the action is the unseen presence of God, creating a pattern that is not immediately evident. The Mexican society that Greene describes is shabby, corrupt and violent, a world that seems 'abandoned', a word repeated often in the opening chapters. The characters are far from heroic, often behaving in petty ways, self-centred, seldom having any dignity. The priest giggles frequently and plays childish card tricks. The action, on the surface, is similar to that of a detective story. A man is wanted by the police, tries to find places to hide, is picked up in a general police raid, but manages to escape. Finally he is tricked out of a secure hiding place, captured and executed.

The way in which the story is told is also similar to the methods of crime fiction. Clues are planted and only followed up later, events are left unexplained, suspense is created during the hunt. *The Power and the Glory* can be read as a story of the shabby modern world, in which men suffer much pain, in which some are always willing to betray others. Read in this way it is a thriller rather similar to some of Greene's 'entertainments'.

At the same time, however, the events can be seen not as a thriller but as a pattern ordained by God. The Red Shirts were waiting to capture the priest if he had taken the boat to Vera Cruz on the day he met Mr Tench and was called to see a sick Indian woman. The Chief of Police complains, 'It was just luck that he didn't catch the boat.' Was it luck or God's plan? The mysterious, unexplained elements may be caused by divine grace. The corruption and decay serve to produce the awareness of sin necessary to redemption. Coral's death is never explained. Is this part of the technique of a thriller? Or is it because God, behind the scenes, used her death as a means of leading the priest towards his execution? And is the execution itself the end of a worthless life, or the beginning of sainthood? Through his technique Greene has created an adventure story in which the 'criminal' is pursued by God.

Style

Graham Greene is a conscious artist with words. He once said that the artist has a duty to be accurate and truthful:

> My characters must not go white in the face or tremble like leaves, not because these phrases are clichés but because they are untrue. This is not only a matter of the artistic conscience but of the social conscience too . . . Every time a phrase like one of these passes into the mind uncriticised, it muddies the stream of thought.*

Greene's style is usually taut. He does not use a great number of descriptive adjectives. The vocabulary is limited by the milieu in which the story is set. Dialogue is normally a series of short, simple sentences. Most of the novel is told in everyday language; even during the philosophical discussions between the priest and the lieutenant the words they choose are primarily concrete and colloquial: 'what a fake'; 'there's one belief we both of us have—that we'll all be dead in a hundred years'; 'you think that stuff won't go down with me'; 'the smallest glass of love mixed with a pint pot of ditch-water'.

Greene does not give elaborate descriptions, but he does use many images, carefully chosen to have wider resonances. Some suggest biblical echoes, without, however, always establishing patterns and without necessarily being serious. Recurring images suggest themes. The images of the universe, presented from the points of view of various characters, indicate differences in their visions. To Padre José this world 'would roll heavily in space under its fog like a burning and abandoned ship'. To the lieutenant the truth is 'a vacant universe and a cooling world'. The Fellows are 'carried through the huge spaces without any knowledge of their destination'.

A favourite stylistic device of Greene's is to compare an abstract quality and a concrete object. Occasionally, the concrete is compared to an abstraction, to show that beyond its everyday significance lies a deeper meaning: 'He drank the brandy down like damnation'. More often the abstract is compared to the concrete, in a simile or a metaphor, in order to give vividness to what are psychological or often theological concepts: 'Terror was always just behind her shoulder'; 'he felt his own unworthiness like a weight at the back of the tongue', 'the

*Elizabeth Bowen, Graham Greene, V.S. Pritchett, *Why Do I Write?*, Percival Marshall, London, 1948, p.30.

world was in her heart like the small spot of decay in a fruit'; 'His conscience . . . was like a slot machine into which any coin could be fitted, even a cheater's blank disk'; 'he could feel his prayers weigh him down like undigested food': 'evil ran like malaria in his veins'. Many of these images serve to make religion concrete, physical. The mystery of the Catholic Mass—the believer does take 'God in the mouth'—is vital to Greene. Man is made in God's image, so God is in all man's physical actions. If there does seem to be a gap between the sordid adventure story told in an often flat style and the significance of the pursuit of the soul by God, it is only an illusion. For Greene the sordid world, not some remote heaven, is the abode of God, and the sinner, although corrupted with human faults, is made in God's image.

Another of Greene's stylistic devices is the use of a list of nouns or a series of images, to convey an atmosphere, a concept, or a person: 'When people confessed to him in terms of passion, was this all they meant—the hard bed and the busy woman and the not talking about the past?' Mr Tench's memories of his talk with the priest are 'a green watering-can, the photo of the children, the cast he was making out of sand for a split palate'. Padre José's wife is reduced to 'a bony shadow within the mosquito-tent, a lanky jaw and a short grey pigtail and an absurd bonnet'.

Since the story is usually presented from the point of view of one of the characters, there is no narrative voice representing the author, making direct judgements on the action. Rather, judgements are indicated indirectly through the imagery or through choice of details. In the description of the night the priest spends in the abandoned farmhouse with the half-caste, many details suggest treachery: 'blackened ground', 'something howled', 'mosquitoes came droning'. The half-caste frequently spits and scratches himself under the armpit, an indication of an uncleanliness which seems moral as well as physical. One of his toes sticks through his shoes, 'plump and yellow like something which lives underground'. Mrs Fellows is similarly judged through a series of physical details. 'a scared thin face', 'she strained away from him towards the wall', she 'rocked backwards and forwards, backwards and forwards', 'she had a handkerchief soaked in eau-de-Cologne over her eyes', 'hunched up under the mosquito-net'. She always speaks either 'sharply' or 'sullenly'.

As does the structure, the style often resembles that of a detective novel. Before the half-caste joins the priest, he appears as a man lying in a hammock. 'The priest said, "*Buenas tardes.*" The man opened his eyes and watched him.' A feeling of suspense, of coming danger is already present in the flat tone with which the apparently harmless and insignificant incident is recounted. Descriptions often create an atmosphere of tension. In Part II, Chapter 4, the priest's flight to the border, many images reinforce the sense of desolation, of impending doom: 'like hate on a deathbed', 'the lightning stabbed down', 'fell to the ground, like the bird offering herself', 'like a dark heap of cattle dung', 'like match-flames through the grass'. Each time the priest encounters the Chief of Police or the lieutenant, the possibility of his discovery exists. Greene varies the way suspense is created. The lieutenant actually looks at the priest's photo while speaking to him in the village, then queries Brigitta about his identity. As the reader knows how unreliable she is, the moment holds considerable tension. The Chief of Police, however, a less dangerous figure, after some time drinking with and talking to the priest, simply says 'Your face somehow'. The sentence, like the thought, is left unfinished. When the priest leaves prison, the lieutenant watches him closely 'as if memory were beginning to work'. The priest then gets caught in a lie about his resemblance to Montez. But the lieutenant remains 'brooding'.

Sources for *The Power and the Glory* in *The Lawless Roads*

The Lawless Roads, the travel book Greene wrote after his trip to Mexico in 1938, includes his impressions of the country, anecdotes about a number of people he met, and his own reactions to the tiring journeys, bad food, heat and violence he experienced or witnessed. Mexico, he felt, still had a spiritual sense: 'Here were idolatry and oppression, starvation and casual violence, but you lived under the shadow of religion—of God or the Devil'. American culture, in contrast, 'wasn't evil, it wasn't anything at all, it was just the drugstore and the Coca Cola, the hamburger, the sinless empty graceless chromium world'.* England, when he returned, seemed unreal:

> Mass in Chelsea seemed curiously fictitious; no peon knelt with his arms out in the attitude of the cross, no woman dragged herself up the aisle on her knees... We do not mortify ourselves. Perhaps we are in need of violence.†

Greene's fascination with the violence of the fight between God and the Devil is evident in *The Power and the Glory*.

In his 1978 introduction to *The Lawless Roads*, Greene says that he had no idea when he returned to England that a novel would come out of his experiences, but that most of the characters in *The Power and the Glory* were based on people he met or heard about in Mexico. He was told of a kindly, disreputable Padre Rey in Panama who had

The Lawless Roads, p.221.
†*The Lawless Roads*, p.272.

married, a source for Padre José. He met a dentist who he says needed no 'touching up' to become Mr Tench, an amiable, corrupt Chief of Police, a half-caste with two yellow fangs, a girl who was educated by correspondence courses from America, a kindly German couple who looked after him. Thus, Greene said, 'I was only handing out alternative destinies to real people whom I had encountered on my journey'.* Greene says, however, that he had to invent the lieutenant, as he had met no one with such integrity among the Mexican police.

For the hero of *The Power and the Glory*, there are several sources. Greene learned about a 'whisky priest' in Chiapas who had been so drunk he baptised a boy 'Brigitta'. The people had told him to go, as they could not protect him. Greene comments: 'He was little loss, poor man, a kind of Padre Rey; but who can judge what terror and hardship and isolation may have excused him in the eyes of God?'† Another source for the hero of *The Power and the Glory* is Father Miguel Pro, who studied in a foreign seminary, returned to Mexico in 1926 disguised in non-clerical clothing, and was shot in a prison yard eighteen months later. During those months, while celebrating many Masses, he cleverly escaped capture by the police several times; once they seized him but did not recognise him and let him go. He was photographed praying for his enemies next to the prison wall before his execution. A third source is a nameless priest in Tabasco who 'existed for ten years in the forests and the swamps, venturing out only at night; his few letters, I was told, recorded an awful sense of impotence—to live in constant danger and yet be able to do so little, it hardly seemed worth the horror.'** In describing his hero's escape across the Chiapas border, Greene also used his own sense of desperation, hunger and fatigue during a mule trip. He was told of a priest who came into Yajalon, in Chiapas, and held a mass baptism, turning away one mother who was fifty centavos short of the rate of two pesos a head:

> It is a depressing fact that persecution does not necessarily produce Father Pros. Any priests who remained in Chiapas were under no control; the Bishop had been banished; there was no court of appeal against a corrupt priest; and who can judge the temptation to such a priest, living in a Godless state ... ? At any moment he might be imprisoned, or banished to join his half-starved brother priests in Mexico City, with nothing to hope for but a good death.‡

In spite of his other failings, however, Greene's priest does not succumb to the temptation to make money from his baptisms.

*The Lawless Roads, p.xiv.
†The Lawless Roads, p.141.
**The Lawless Roads, p.121.
‡The Lawless Roads, p.188.

Greene thus combines the struggles of the priest who remained with the vices of the whisky priest, the temptations of the priest in Yajalon, his own tiring journey, and the martyrdom of Miguel Pro, to make his fictional character. He deliberately foregoes the saintly gestures of Pro (which are instead almost mocked in the parody story of Juan the Martyr); the hero of *The Power and the Glory* is a weak man who seems to say 'Excuse', not pray for his persecutors. He is full of vices, because Greene wanted to show both that the weakness of the man does not detract from the power of the priest and also that the sinner is close to God.

Hints for study

Points for detailed study

The plot of *The Power and the Glory* may be hard to follow, as various strands are juxtaposed, with breaks in the action and with characters not always identified when they appear. Re-read the novel carefully, referring to these notes. Then practise writing on the following topics.

1. *Themes*
(*a*) What happens in the novel to suggest that the priest may be a saint? What alternate, naturalistic explanations are given for these events?
(*b*) List the main arguments about man and society between the priest and the lieutenant. (How do they differ in their assessment of human nature? What different goals do they have?)
(*c*) What does Greene satirise in Mexican society? Find specific incidents satirising, for example, piety or materialism.

2. *Characters*
Write sketches of the following characters in the novel: Padre José, Captain Fellows, Coral, the Chief of Police, the half-caste. List their personal characteristics and how they are presented. Identify his or her function in terms of the plot and the themes. Does the character suggest a parallel or contrast to other characters?

3. *Style*
List examples of metaphors and similes. What do they convey?

4. *Structure*
Outline the structure of the novel, indicating sudden breaks, various points of view and the use of suspense.

Illustrative quotations

You should be able to identify significant passages in the novel and comment upon them. Here are three quotations and short sample comments.

1. The priest's dilemma

If he left them, they would be safe, and they would be free from his example. He was the only priest the children could remember: it was from him they would take their ideas of the faith. But it was from him too they took God—in their mouths. When he was gone it would be as if God in all this space between the sea and the mountains ceased to exist. Wasn't it his duty to stay, even if they despised him, even if they were murdered for his sake? even if they were corrupted by his example? He was shaken with the enormity of the problem . . . He raised the brandy to his mouth.

Comment: While in Brigitta's village the priest thinks of the reasons for leaving Tabasco and the reasons for staying. The phrase 'took God—in their mouths' is typical of the physical manner in which Greene describes faith. At this point, early in the novel, the priest still has some pride. Typically, when he cannot think clearly, he starts to drink.

Man in God's image

But at the centre of his own faith there always stood the convincing mystery—that we were made in God's image. God was the parent, but He was also the policeman, the criminal, the priest, the maniac, and the judge. Something resembling God dangled from the gibbet or went into odd attitudes before the bullets in a prison yard or contorted itself like a camel in the attitude of sex.

Comment: The priest takes the biblical saying that man was created in God's image literally; not only is man like God in his spirit but in his body. Thus he imagines God dying, God having sexual relations. Most Christians would think such an interpretation absurd; to the priest, however, it is a way of seeing the divine in all life, even the most sordid, and therefore a path towards the love of his fellow men. Two of his examples—the attitude of sex and the prison yard—refer to his own life, one from the past, one a prediction of his death. There is a hint of disgust with sexual activity in the phrase 'contorted itself like a camel'.

3. The execution

Of course there was nothing to do. Everything went very quickly like a routine. The officer stepped aside, the rifles went up, and the little man suddenly made jerky movements with his arms. He was trying to say something: what was the phrase they were always supposed to use? That was routine too, but perhaps his mouth was too dry, because nothing came out except a word that sounded like 'Excuse'.

Comment: The priest's death, as seen from a distance by Mr Tench, is neither dramatic, nor heroic. It is merely 'routine'. The priest is only a 'little man' who makes 'jerky movements'. Rather than praying for his persecutors, like Juan the Martyr, he seems to be begging their pardon. If his mouth was too dry, it is possibly the result of drink. Mr Tench is incapable of any action. 'Of course there was nothing to do'.

Writing an examination answer or essay on *The Power and the Glory*

A good essay or examination answer should: (*a*) Answer the specific question and not bring in irrelevant material. (*b*) Be well organised. Begin with a statement of what you intend to show. Then divide your material into paragraphs, in each of which you include a clear topic sentence stating the theme of the paragraph. Finally, write a short conclusion, bringing your various points together. (*c*) Show detailed and useful knowledge of the text. Bring in specific examples of incidents and characters. Give quotations when possible. Remember you are writing about a novel, not an illustration of a theological theme. Consider humour and irony. Do not, however, bring in miscellaneous information, for example about Greene's trip to Mexico, unless it supports an argument you wish to make and has a direct bearing on the novel.

Study the following sample answers as examples of how to organise material.

Sample questions and answers

1. Discuss how Greene's choice of characters in *The Power and the Glory* helps to illustrate his themes.

The Power and the Glory is concerned with the omnipresence of God in daily life, and the mysterious power of God's grace, of which the sinner is often more aware than the good man. Through the lives of the characters, and implied parallels and contrasts among them, the novel illustrates these themes.

While *The Power and the Glory* may appear on the surface as an adventure story, God's presence can be seen in the lives of a group of ordinary, sometimes disreputable people. Those who are not Catholic —such as Trixie Fellows and Mr Tench—often feel 'abandoned', without a purpose. After meeting the priest Coral begins to think about God. Even the lieutenant starts to question his previous convictions. Those who are Catholics are often aware of grace trying to reach them. James Calver writes a note to the priest to come 'for Christ's sake'. Even the half-caste begs the priest to pray for him.

The sinner is directly aware of God. Padre José, weak and cowardly as he is, realises the enormity of his sin in God's eyes, and feels the mocking children may be an inversion of a choir of angels calling him to repent. Comparing himself to Calver and the prisoners, feeling unworthy, the whisky priest, through humility, comes closer to God. Sinners are contrasted to the pious women, such as Luis's mother or the good woman in prison, who seem blind to the real presence of God and who try to reduce religion to sentimental stories and holy images.

Contrasts among characters often show the difference between those whose desires are centred upon the material world and those who think about the essential meaning of life. Padre José's wife, interested in sex and her pension, is contrasted with her husband. The Chief of Police, only concerned with drink and his toothache, is contrasted with the lieutenant. Brigitta, a tough, prematurely wise village child is contrasted with Coral, aware of her responsibilities and questioning the weakness of her parents' values.

The major character contrast is between the priest and the lieutenant. The lieutenant leads a good life and is dedicated to a cause. The priest is dissolute, alcoholic and unsure of what to do. In spite of his weakness, however, he is chosen by God, and the lieutenant is left feeling empty, with no goal to pursue.

Without directly stating that God is influencing the thoughts of his characters, Greene suggests a mysterious divine presence in daily life. He contrasts those who are aware of this presence and the often weak and insignificant characters who ignore it. The novel shows that God is present in our shabby, corrupted world, and that the only worthy goal of man is to try 'to be a saint'.

---

2. A frequent criticism of Graham Greene's fiction is that he is 'unfair to his characters', presenting those with whom he disagrees in a partial and biased way. Would you agree that he is 'unfair' to the lieutenant in *The Power and the Glory*?

The lieutenant in *The Power and the Glory* is, from a Catholic perspective, an instrument of the Devil, seeking to destroy all vestiges of faith in Mexico. If the novel were simply religious propaganda, he might be presented as a totally evil person. If the novel were strictly objective, only showing the actions of the characters and never judging them, the lieutenant would be presented as a strong man, who succeeds in reaching his goal. Greene has chosen to present his character in a more complex fashion, seeing his qualities as well as his failings. He does, however, indicate clearly that from his own perspective the lieutenant is wrong; he suggests that God may be trying to change him.

The lieutenant is seen as admirable in many ways. We sympathise with him because he suffered from poverty in his childhood. Correctly, it is implied, he thought of the Church hierarchy as a suppressor of the peasants. He is a dedicated man, lives austerely and never thinks of personal gain. He is often generous, giving money to the priest when he thinks he is a poor man. He breaks the law by trying to get Padre José to hear the priest's confession and by bringing illegal brandy to the death cell. He has a certain nobility in his willingness to accept a meaningless universe and his desire nevertheless to fight for a better life for the children of Mexico. During the discussion between the priest and the lieutenant, while his sympathies are obviously with the priest, Greene gives the lieutenant some strong arguments about the need to alleviate suffering.

Greene does, however, influence our emotional reactions to the lieutenant by the manner in which he is described. The lieutenant has 'an air of bitter distaste' for the corruption around him. His bitterness and austerity, often emphasised, make him seem almost inhuman: 'He had the dignity of an idea, standing in the little whitewashed room with his polished boots and his venom.' He can only see people in the abstract; he is incapable of love for any individual. While he seems to respect the priest as a man, he is determined to kill him for his ideas.

In suggesting that the lieutenant is disturbed after the priest's execution, Greene perhaps seems unfair to his character. Greene could, we may feel, have left the lieutenant sure of his own position and not cast doubt on his strength of purpose. There is also mockery in the style in which the lieutenant's last thoughts are described: 'the dynamic love which used to move his trigger-finger felt flat and dead'. The lieutenant's love is shown to be hatred. While Greene often shows respect for the lieutenant, and never treats him with the broad satire used for Padre José's wife and Trixie Fellows, he finally rejects his character in what may seem an 'unfair' manner.

---

3. How does the narrative method of *The Power and the Glory* influence the reader's appraisal of the whisky priest?

In *The Power and the Glory* Greene portrays a weak, cowardly, confused man who is pursued by the police, to whom he is a dangerous enemy, and by God, who uses him for a divine purpose. The problem for the novelist is to make this character credible as a human being, while allowing for the mystery of God's grace to operate. The priest's life is not admirable, yet the reader must also understand that the priest can fulfil a function in the community of believers.

One way of making the characterisation of the whisky priest work is to show him at a distance, so that the reader sees him as others do. In both Part I and Part IV of the novel the priest is presented largely through the opinions of others. Mr Tench sees him as a small man with bad teeth who seems to want to escape from Tabasco; Luis's mother sees him as a disgrace to the Church; the lieutenant sees him as a last enemy to be eliminated. At the end of the novel, however, Mr Tench is horrified by the execution, and Luis's mother proclaims that the priest is a saint. One effect of this narrative structure is to make the reader see the priest as initially an insignificant figure but one whose death has suddenly given him a new stature, a meaning that extends beyond the personal to the community.

In the central sections of the novel Greene often presents the perspective of the priest. He does not portray him as an heroic figure or even one who can think clearly about his problems. Often, wondering what to do next, the priest begins to drink. His dreams are confused mixtures of religious symbols and past events. He is strangely attracted to an adolescent girl who helps him. He giggles often. He is not brave before his execution.

Greene does not, however, destroy the reader's sympathy for the priest. The priest offers himself as a hostage in the village. He tries to be kind to the prisoners. He returns to the dead Indian child to see if the mother needs help. He refuses to make much money from baptisms. He even promises to pray for the half-caste. He accuses himself of pride; but he has lost all pride by the time he goes to prison. His sins are rather those that the modern reader would not strongly condemn: drunkenness, fornication.

Through a structure showing the priest both from the outside and from the inside, and through a portrayal stressing certain weaknesses but subtly showing virtues of love, Greene directs the reader's response so that we can believe the whisky priest has become a martyr and a saint.

---

4. In *The Lawless Roads* Greene wrote about Mexico: 'Here were idolatry and oppression . . . but you lived under the shadow of religion —of God or the Devil.' Discuss the significance of the Mexican setting in *The Power and the Glory*.

The Power and the Glory is set in Mexico, a land of violent contrasts and enduring faith. There are corrupt government officials, much bribery, frequent betrayal, oppression of the poor, discrimination against the Indians and casual violence—the murder of an innocent Indian child, for example. There are also violent storms, famine, extreme heat, poor soil, disease and mosquitoes. It is a world where men are vicious and where nature is cruel.

Often the novel conveys specific details of Mexican life. Greene portrays the superstitions of the Mexican, happy to kiss the priest's gloved hand and to collect holy pictures and bogus relics. The Indians, set apart from modern society, have their own strong but exotic religion, a blend of earlier faith and Christianity. The novel describes the sense of physical isolation in Tabasco, with few roads and difficult access to the sea, and captures the atmosphere of a small provincial town, with Sunday evening promenades, beer and *gaseosa*.

What matters most to Greene, however, is that in Mexico the supernatural is a part of everyday life; religion is not merely a Sunday ritual. The peasants may be superstitious, but they realise that God matters. Mexico was also, in the 1930s, a land where the force of the Devil seemed at work through the official government policy of suppressing religion. Thus Mexico was an ideal setting for a story about the mysterious presence of God in the shabby and corrupt everyday world and about the call of grace, even or especially to the weakest of sinners.

Part 5

Suggestions for further reading

The text

The Power and the Glory, The Collected Edition of Graham Greene, with an introduction by the author, Volume 5, William Heinemann and The Bodley Head, London, 1971.

The Power and the Glory, Penguin Books, Harmondsworth, 1971.

The Power and the Glory, Bantam Books, The Viking Press, New York, 1967.

Other works by Graham Greene

The Collected Edition of Graham Greene, William Heinemann and The Bodley Head, London, 1970– . Contains Greene's works with new introductions by the author; of special interest to the student of *The Power and the Glory* is Volume 19, *The Lawless Roads*, 1978.

The Collected Essays of Graham Greene, The Bodley Head, London, 1969. Contains 'The Lost Childhood', about Greene's own childhood, a selection of his reviews of the work of other novelists, and other essays.

A Sort of Life, The Bodley Head, London, 1971. Greene's autobiography up to 1932.

Ways of Escape, The Bodley Head, London, 1980. Continuation of Greene's autobiography.

Most of Graham Greene's works are also available in paperback editions published by Penguin Books, Harmondsworth. They include the travel books, *The Lawless Roads* and *Journey Without Maps*; *A Sort of Life*; the following novels: *Brighton Rock*, *It's a Battlefield*, *Our Man in Havana*, *The Heart of the Matter*, *The Comedians*, *A Burnt-Out Case*, *The End of the Affair*, *The Honorary Consul*, *The Ministry of Fear*, *The Quiet American*, and *Travels with My Aunt*.

Works on Greene

ALLOTT, KENNETH, AND FARRIS, MIRIAM: *The Art of Graham Greene*, Russell & Russell, New York, 1963. First published in 1951 and one of the earliest studies of Greene, this only discusses his work up to *The Heart of the Matter*.

ATKINS, JOHN: *Graham Greene*, Calder & Boyars, London, revised edition, 1966. A rather opinionated study with anti-Catholic bias, but makes some interesting critical points.

HYNES, SAMUEL (ED): *Graham Greene. A Collection of Critical Essays*, Prentice-Hall, Englewood Cliffs, New Jersey, 1973. In addition to containing a number of useful essays on Greene, this volume includes two interviews with Greene.

KUNKEL, FRANCIS L.: *The Labyrinthine Ways of Graham Greene*, Paul P. Appel, Mamaroneck, New York, 1973. This study, from a Roman Catholic viewpoint, is especially valuable on the characters and the symbols in Greene's fiction.

LEWIS, R.W.B., AND CONN, PETER J.: *The Power and the Glory*, The Viking Press, New York, 1970. The text of the novel is followed by a good selection of critical essays and some of Greene's own essays that are useful for an understanding of the novel.

LODGE, DAVID: *Graham Greene*, Columbia Essays on Modern Writers, Columbia University Press, New York, 1966. A good introduction to Greene's work and his place in contemporary literature.

PRYCE-JONES, DAVID: *Graham Greene*, Writers and Critics, Oliver and Boyd, Edinburgh, 1963. A useful introduction to Greene's work.

TURNELL, MARTIN: *Graham Greene: A Critical Essay*, Contemporary Writers in Christian Perspective series, William Eerdmans, Grand Rapids, Michigan, 1967. Provides a useful commentary on Greene's fiction, while discussing how his religious vision is personal and differs from traditional Christian belief.

The author of these notes

ADELE KING was educated at the University of Iowa, the University of Leeds, and the Sorbonne. She has taught French in the United States, Canada, England and Nigeria, and she held an American Association of University Women Postdoctoral Fellowship in 1977–8 for research into the work of Camara Laye. Her publications include *Camus, Proust, Paul Nizan: écrivain*, and *The Writings of Camara Laye*; she is also author of York Notes on Hemingway's *A Farewell to Arms*, Ibsen's *Ghosts*, Camus' *L'Etranger*, and Laye's *L'Enfant Noir*.